VILLAGE VOICES

Village Voices

The Witham Friary History Project
2015

First published 2015 by Withambooks
© Witham Friary History Project
Foreword © Andrew Miller

www.withamfriary.org.uk/history

ISBN 978-0-9934164-0-8

British Library Cataloguing in Publication Data
A catalogue record for this book is available for the British Library

Book design by Chris Chapman: zulspr@icloud.com
Printed by Short Run Press, Exeter

Front cover photograph:
Saturday, April 26th, 1975. During a quiet spell in his afternoon shift
at Witham signal box, using a 1915 Taylor Hobson lens on his camera,
Adrian Vaughan recorded this idyllic scene from the railway bridge
Opposite half title:
Pete Douel before his first day at Selwood School, Frome,
with a strawberry roan cow in the Seymour Arms yard. September 1970
Rear cover photographs:
top right – Silver Jubilee celebrations in the pub garden. Tuesday, June 7th, 1977
bottom left – Alison Kefford in Windleys, early nineteen-seventies

CONTENTS

FOREWORD 6

PREFACE 8

THE TRANSCRIPTS 11

GLOSSARY OF LOCAL TERMS 132

CONTRIBUTORS & PHOTOGRAPHY CREDITS 133

INDEX 134

FOREWORD

This short, lovely book is a series of conversations with men and women in their seventh, eighth or ninth decades. Country men and country women, some of them farmers, some born in the village, with memories stretching back to the Second World War and beyond. The village itself is the kind of place people often refer to as remote but remote from what? It is not remote from fields and farms and woods and great estates. Roman roads criss-cross the parish; a great monastery was founded in what is now a sheep field by a man later raised to the company of saints.

Viewed from above – the temporal 'above' as well as the spatial – it is a palimpsest of maps, dense with tracks, the lost foundations of great houses and small ones, of water courses and short cuts, boundary lines, named fields (which have a poetry of their own), and all those places where once something happened, or probably happened, events living on in webs of story that are, of course, another kind of map and as important as any.

We learn from these pages a great deal about the social and economic history of the last hundred years though it is left to us, the readers, to sift and delve and take from stray remarks the larger picture. Or we can, if we prefer, simply sit at an imagined fireside and listen to them, West Country voices, some ready enough to talk, others needing the gentle coaxing of the interviewers. An event – some bare hour stubborn against oblivion – is recalled in close detail; a little later and two sentences suffice to swing through half a life. It's how we speak, how we remember. Names appear, a clutch of them recurring again and again, old families, usually farming families. Others are mentioned just once, as if surfacing briefly out of the river of history itself.

Don Stevens at Moorpark Farm, circa 1936:
"There's my lamb. I did jump on his back an' hang on an' go for a ride. Hee hee hee!"

How much has changed? How much remains the same? The cows are still cows, though new breeds have come and old ones disappeared. The physical village has been added to but not overwhelmingly, and if you trudge past the pub and under the railway bridge you are out onto the same single lane track between high hedges that would have been familiar to those who walked it long before the first tractors arrived on the land. As for the pub – stone floors, stopped clock, a rack of hand-painted Victorian beer pumps – it has been in the same family for three generations.

But the changes are real enough, and profound. The pre-war village was a scraped back place for many: houses where interior plumbing meant a single cold-water tap over a Belfast sink, the toilet a wooden seat over a bucket. The last of the outlying farms were connected to the National Grid in the early nineteen-sixties. Now street lamps light the turnings of the road; and broadband, however sluggish, feeds computers in rooms where, well within living memory, there was only the glow of paraffin lamps, the flicker of a candle.

The war itself appears as a kind of fault line running through these stories. Agricultural work was a reserved occupation, so men who would otherwise have been conscripted to fight, remained – with mixed emotions? – on their farms to feed a nation struggling for its survival. Military life meant the Home Guard and later, in the run up to D–Day, the presence of GIs in the pub (a remarkable footnote in Roy Wheeler's reminiscences concerning the sad state of race relations in the US army). It's strange and instructive how the great events of those years had their small though not unimportant echoes in the life of the village – a stray bomb falling into a fishpond, a chess set carved by a German POW and given as a gift one Christmas; a dead British pilot in the cockpit of his Hurricane (*"He looked perfect, wasn't shot about or anything like that…"*).

The winter of '47; the winter of '63. Snow so deep it lay level with the platforms of the now long-since abolished railway station. People remember the cold, the digging and scraping, the heroic tractors, the patient cows slithering across frozen yards to the parlours…

In the nineteen-fifties much of the parish was sold off at auction. It had belonged to the Dukes of Somerset, was part of their estate, and handed to the auctioneer to raise money for death duties. In Witham Friary the feudal world is not a hopelessly remote thing. Water for the village still comes from springs on the Duke's land and villagers send their cheques for water to the ducal office at Berry Pomeroy. The figure of the Duke (one or other of them) makes a scatter of cameo appearances in these pages, perhaps descending to the vale as part of a shooting party, crossing the land of one of his tenants. Relations seem to have been amicable enough, though one senses the villagers – not just the farmers – had always a streak of that West Country anarchism that gave rise in other times to burnings, riot and rebellion.

One of the most touching aspects of these interviews – an aspect that is as much a part of a subtly shifting cultural history as any mention of mechanisation or changing patterns of employment – is the recollection of a half-dozen or so country courtships. The Friday night dances, the borrowing of cars, the outings, the need to be home for second milking. The sheer slowness of it! Months of visiting before anything was said or declared. Then the quiet establishing of marriages that (have) lasted for decades and were expected to. Love stories set in a landscape; romances never much separated from the world of work and necessity.

A.M. Fox Cottage 2015

PREFACE

Probably named from the Anglo-Saxon, meaning 'homestead of Witta' and a corruption of the French word *frerie* 'brotherhood', Witham Friary is mentioned in the Domesday Book as supporting eleven people. The first Carthusian Priory was established here in an attempt by Henry II to appease the Church for the murder of Thomas Becket. Built by Hugh, arguably one of the greatest figures of his time, who became the Bishop of Lincoln and later raised to the Communion of Saints. The Priory did not survive the dissolution of the monasteries although the lay brothers chapel became the parish church. Also associated with the Priory, and currently an architect's office, the fourteenth century dovecot was used as the village lock-up after the demolition of the Red Lion Inn. It then became two tenements, then the village reading room before becoming the parish room. In 1901 the Duke of Somerset commissioned a restoration of the building and its original use became apparent – more than one thousand pigeonholes were discovered.

After the dissolution of Witham Priory the lands and privileges were granted to Ralph Hopton. Witham became a Peculiar over which the Bishop had no authority, allowing Hopton to appoint and dismiss curates and even to prove the wills of parishioners at a local court. The Hoptons converted the monastery buildings into a residence but the Wyndhams (to whom Ralph Hopton bequeathed the Manor of Witham) turned it into a stately mansion in the Palladian style. Alderman William Beckford was the next owner in 1762, a well-known political figure renowned for his interest in British civil liberty despite being the biggest slave owner in Jamaica. Beckford had a new house designed but died during building. His son – whose properties included Fonthill Manor and Beckford's Tower – couldn't afford to complete the work so the building was dismantled and the materials sold.

The most interesting of the old houses was the Red Lion Inn, run by the Mussell family. It stood near the church in three sides of a square, containing the brew house, the blind house (village prison), the club room, the dwelling house, a dairy and taproom, together with a courtyard paved with flagstones where the villagers used to dance on festival days. The club room and brew house were demolished in 1867 and the main building was converted into the teacher's house and two cottages, still extant. William Munday of the Red Lion became the first landlord of the Seymour Arms, completed in 1856. It still flourishes today, run by the descendants of William Salvidge who took it over in the 1880s. The school was built in 1838 by the Duke of Somerset; previously a little education had been provided in conjunction with the Sunday school. In 1859 the church band of minstrels – as in Hardy's Mellstock – was displaced by an organ. The parish agreed to levy an educational rate and to provide a teacher who would also play the organ in the church. Although the school closed in 1965, the venue still plays an important part in village life as the village hall.

In the middle of the nineteenth century the weekly agricultural wage to married men was eight shillings a week. Daily food was bread, potatoes, butter and cheese – 'pot cakes' or barley 'bannocks' often took the place of bread. Bacon was the usual meat diet. Their meagre income was augmented by growing their own produce, being allowed to glean from harvest fields, keeping a pig whose feed was supplemented by turnips and mangolds given by the generosity of farmers, often with half the finished pig being sold off to pay for the salt for curing the other half. Farming and forestry have always been the main activities in Witham but evidence exists that an iron industry flourished here from the Middle Ages. Silk manufacture took place in cottages in The Yard; bricks and tiles were made at Upper Holt until the start of the First World War.

The baptism register to which Reverend E.B.Prince refers in his 1909 pamphlet tell us of Witham life in the nineteenth century. He quotes:

'On examining this book one is struck at once by the unbroken line of family life which has been preserved in the Parish; you find one hundred years ago the familiar names of Crees, Hughes, Stride, Macey, Hallett, Stickler, Edwards, Ashford, Bown, Hoddinott, Croom, etc., etc. – you notice also the disappearance of many old families, such as Battels, Pitman, Urch, etc., as well as the disappearance of many trades, e.g., cordwainer, spade-tree maker, tailor, etc., etc'.

He also comments on the marriage register:

*"The first thing you notice is that in the early days of the century nearly all marriages were between persons actually resident in the Parish of Witham. The boys and girls grew up together, and were satisfied to make their homes among their own people – a very happy arrangement, if somewhat simple and primitive – to be accounted for no doubt by the isolated character of the Parish, for after the opening of the Railway this feature of social life gradually disappears. The next thing that attracts attention is that so many signatures were made with the mark **X**. In several instances the contracting parties, as well as the witnesses, were unable to write their own names. No better evidence of the result of improved education can be found than by a reference to this book. The progress was gradual, but sure. After 1880 only one or two entries occur in which the **X** was used – now all are able to write."*

As Reverend Prince noted, the railway opening in 1856 changed the parish for ever, for now was added to the old rural population the men who worked on the line and the staff at the station. The station closed one hundred years later in 1966, a victim of the Beeching axe. The railway remains open but only freight trains stop at Witham now, waiting for a 'path' to carry roadstone from Merehead Quarry to Westbury and beyond. We will leave the twentieth century history to those residents of the parish, past and present, who so generously gave their time to enable us to produce this book, the idea for which was conceived whilst beating the bounds on Rogation Sunday, 2011. The final word to Reverend Prince, curiously prescient of today:

"So good-bye to the old Witham! Good-bye to the old names, the old customs, the old follies, the old sorrows. The Witham of the twentieth century may be more outwardly decent, better paid, better clothed, better housed, better fed, but no advantages will compensate for the loss of that which made the past so valuable – I mean that spirit of kindliness and sympathy which bound together the rich and the poor, and that fear of God which made Religion a reality, the Bible a delight, and Worship a privilege!

The pen drops from my trembling fingers, and the pale mists of this new century creep up and hide the past once more!"

19 35 WITHAM FRIARY C.E. SCH. SOMERSET.

The Scholastic Souvenir Company of Blackpool employed agents across the country to take school photographs. In 1935, possibly because it was Jubilee year for King George V, one such agent arrived at Witham and took this souvenir portrait. Violet Stevens of Moorpark Farm, now 86, is the girl seated bottom right: *"We used to play marbles on the way to school, sometimes a spinning top and whip. Didn't start til I was nearly 6. I hated it to begin with. I walked down from Moorpark to the Lodge and on to school with Arthur Salvidge who lived there. Children walked everywhere then. When it was wet Arthur's parents took us down to school with their cob and trap. This is the front yard of the school; the girls and the little ones played there. It was gravel then — we often used to go home with skinned knees. The boys played in the yard to the side of the school by the cottages. We girls used to walk around Red Lion Cottages to play with the boys in their yard until the teachers spotted us!"*

The Transcripts

Stella & John Hill, 72

Dead easy, Buttercup…

Stella was born in Witham.
John came here at the age of fifteen.
They married at Frome Registry Office in 1961.
Apart from a year in Nunney,
they've been here ever since.

I was born at 42 Witham Friary on the 29th of May 1942, a one-up, one-down which is now part of Red Lion Cottage. As far as I can recall we only had cold water in no. 42: I can remember my mum having a black range. The toilet was just the old wooden seat with a hole in and a bucket. The school was exactly the same with only cold water. My parents were the first to move in at Littlewoods, the first council houses in the village to be built after the war. We moved on my fifth birthday. It was very nice; we had all the mod cons, hot water, cold water, running toilets, everything.

I bet your mother couldn't believe it.

No, no and the rent [to the council] at the time was thirteen shillings and a sixpence per week. I went to school at five in the local school next door with Mrs Cunnington, who was then Miss Hunt, the headmistress.

Stella photographed in front of Witham school, now the village hall, in 1947

Stella and her mum at Littlewoods, summer 1947

Where did you go when you finished at Witham Friary school?

Sunny Hill Girls School in Bruton, on the train. I passed the eleven-plus so I went to the girls only school. It was ninety percent private and around ten percent state. If you passed your eleven-plus you went to either Sunny Hill or Frome Grammar School. There was a grammar school in Frome then. But Mrs Cunnington wanted me to go to Bruton.

Did the railway station closing in 1966 affect you?

Well by that time quite a few people had cars. To be truthful, really and truthfully the cars killed the trains off, 'cos everybody had cars and some preferred the coaches. I know Mr Beeching did his terrible worst, but we had cars and vehicles so it was easy. The trouble with the station, especially Frome, was that it was a heck of a long way to walk with your groceries [from the town to the station]. Like I say, there was a butcher who used to come around, there was a greengrocer who used to come around, and Mr Taylor in the village shop, down opposite the church used to do his bit with his bread and his groceries. There was a coach that came up from Baltonsborough, through Evercreech, Westcombe,

Batcombe, Upton Noble, here, Truddoxhill, Tytherington and into Frome, three days a week; three times a day on a Wednesday and a Saturday, and one on a Sunday for the pictures, but then it got less and less. We're now down to one bus weekly.

How did the elderly people fare?

They always managed. If anybody had a problem somebody would do the shopping for them. A doctor would come once a week. If you had somebody poorly or you weren't feeling well you went to Mrs Phelps at no. 45. On Fridays the doctor would call into Mrs Phelps and then he would see whoever was poorly.

Mrs Phelps, was she medically trained?

No, no, she was just the lady who took the messages for the doctor, "Please will you call?"

Not many people had phones.

No, I wouldn't think so; it was years before we had one.

So you lived at the top of Littlewoods first?

Yes, and when we got married I moved into a caravan at Upton Noble. John worked at Millers Farm, and then we moved back to the cottage at no. 44, John working for the Jowett family. Then we moved to Nunney for a year and then back to Witham, to no. 8 [Littlewoods], and now we're here [at Yew Close]. We've been here for twenty five years I think it is.

John: I wasn't a child when I came here in 1956. I was fifteen years old and had left school and had begun work on a farm. From [then] all the young lads had motorbikes, which I always reckon put the nail in the

The summer of '59. Pictured outside Littlewoods, here is John on his James Captain motorbike next to Stella's cousin Maurice Cox on his Ariel Leader. Looking on from her front garden is Vi Cox, Maurice's mother

coffin of the railways. Everybody got wheels; I only used the railways about three times myself – once to take Stella to hospital when we were having a baby.

Stella: February the seventh, 1963.

John: 1963. With the bad weather we were all cut off here and no ambulance couldn't get out to Witham. I didn't fancy taking her in the tractor and trailer – there was talk of a helicopter coming to take her up, which I thought was rather exciting but unfortunately they had stopped the train. Stella says we walked from Frome station to the hospital, but I can't remember that. Heavily pregnant and we walked all the way from Frome station.

Was it the express to London Paddington that stopped [especially for you] at Witham?

John: Yeah, it was the express train.

Stella: Everybody looking out the windows [thinking], why is the train stopping at Witham Friary station?

What did you have?

Stella: A daughter, a second daughter. That evening, actually. Four days later they decided that they would bring me home and that they didn't want to keep me in hospital, so the ambulance slid nearly all the way back to Witham Friary from Frome! We had a pathway by then and needed a big digger to bulldoze the snow out the way. It was pretty bad.

Tell us about your early life on the farm, John.

John: I started at Witham Park Farm at the top of the hill, with Mr Cary. I lived in up there and being a townie I though that was rather strange. We milked the cows with a machine up there, we had a little engine that made the vacuum and that was it; there was no electric on the farm other than that. Calor gas heating and lighting downstairs and we all had our little candlesticks to go to bed with at night. We carried hot water upstairs to bathe, because the plumbing wouldn't carry hot water, we carried two huge buckets of scalding boiling water upstairs and into the bath, we would have a candle light at each end of the bath and that was it.

Did you have tractors?

John: Oh yes, it was quite a modern International which only Peter, the bosses' son, drove. I wasn't allowed to touch that. And, you know, I'm not sure how many cows we milked, but they all had names, they all had horns in those days, tied them up by the neck for milking.

Were they all the same breed?

John: No, they were all sorts. Friesian, shorthorns…

But not Holstein?

John: No, no.

Stella: They weren't invented then.

John: The Carys were…it was quite hard for me from the town. I never touched a cow before but I soon learnt after being kicked when I first tried to milk a cow, pulled the wrong one and she kicked me all across the stall and Mr Cary came down and said "No, that wasn't the one I wanted you to do, I meant the one next door" – he was old fashioned – they still carried the milk with the yoke, do you know what the yoke is? They had to shorten the chains on it so I could pick up the milk; I was only knee high to a grasshopper then. And, um, unfortunately with the snow and the ice one day, I slipped over and dropped the milk, which didn't go down very well. All hard work really for me, to start with, but you got used to it. All in churns, which you would take up to Gare Hill for the lorries to pick up. They still had an old working horse up there, retired, called Janet.

Yes, because you were talking about…

Arthur Cox (Stella's father) pictured here outside West Barn Cottage during his courting years, about to cycle over to Evercreech to see Kitty

Stella: Smart and Flower. My dad was the carter for the Butler family at West Barn [Farm]. If I can remember rightly, my dad's wages, when I was small, the earliest I can remember was two pounds a week. It was all he got.

Two pounds a week and a house?

Stella: And milk. But the rent was thirteen [shillings] and six [pence]. There wasn't much left.

John: I started off with four pounds a week but half that was taken off for board and lodgings, so I was left with two pounds a week. I didn't have any wheels then; later on I had a bicycle and would cycle to youth club and the pictures in Frome.

Stella: And that's how we met.

You met at Witham youth club?

Stella: Mmm.

John: Guess where that was, Deborah?

In the Dovecot. What facilities did you have there?

John: It was just, oh we had a little snooker table. Sometimes we would have table tennis down there and a chap came down there to teach us how to box one day.

Stella: And Anne Phelps, she used to teach us how to do needlecraft.

John: The chap who came to teach us how to box, he said to one lad: "Go on then George, put the gloves on" – so George put the gloves on and then the chap said "come at me." He traded with George, a really tough bloke, [who] just flattened him in one go. We had to pick our instructor up! George don't live around here anymore. He was a strong lad. When we used to go to Frome, cos Frome was pretty rough in those days, nobody messed with George. The Frome lads soon got to know him. That always stuck in my mind, makes me laugh – little cocky bloke that guy was, so George put him in his place. That was about it really. We did music every now and again.

How many attended youth club – was it just youngsters from Witham?

Stella: Just Witham really – there were quite a few youngsters in the village at the time, a couple of families at the top of the hill and a few in the village and at the other end. There seemed to be quite a few teenagers at the time, quite a few motorbikes for the boys; yeah, it wasn't too bad at all

really. You made your own entertainment; it wasn't watching television or playing with the Xbox. Our girls, even when they were growing up, they would go out in the morning and you wouldn't see them until tea time. You'd be afraid to do it now, so…

John: That's why you gave up cooking Sunday dinner, wasn't it? Because they were out…

Stella: They were out and he was at the pub – ooh, I shouldn't say that on this [recording], should I? *(laughs)*

Tell us about the Seymour Arms.

John: Well I was fifteen and a half when I first went in. You weren't supposed to but we did. I remember once when one of the local lads was in there, I was sat behind the door, and he said "Oh, Bill's outside" and Bill was the policeman!

He was the village bobby?

John: Well, he came from Nunney. He was stationed there, and he had this motorbike [Velocette LE] which you couldn't hear coming. So when Bill pulled up outside I thought "Crikey!" I must have been about sixteen then, I had a big pint in my hand and he didn't show himself to me. All of a sudden his head came around the door and he says "Alright young man?" and I said "Yes, thank you." Because I wasn't causing any trouble he didn't bother me. Nowadays you would get in trouble for drinking underage. If I was a trouble maker they would have turfed me out.

Stella: There never has been any trouble in the village pub anyway, at all.

John: A few spats maybe but nothing serious.

WITHAM FOOTBALL CLUB.
1927-8

Mr ARYALL, P. CLARK, A.G. EDWARDS, R. JAMES, H. NICHOLLS, H. SALVIGE, W. SARGENT, Mr H. HODDINOTT.

M. YOEMAN, F. GALE, G. RYALL, C. ANDREWS, J. NICHOLLS.
(VICE CAPTAIN) (CAPTAIN.)

The Witham football team photographed outside the dovecot, presumably at the start of the season in September 1927. In the back row is Herb Salvidge, having returned safe from the Great War trenches apart from some 'scrapnel' in his leg, later to become landlord of the Seymour Arms. Within eight years of this photograph being taken Fred Gale (Vice Captain) will become father to Duncan. Reg James lived at No. 4 Holt Cottages and later worked at Colemans quarry

Have you seen the black and white photograph of the football team in the pub, Deborah?

Oh yes, I've seen it.

John: Well, Herbert Salvidge is in that picture *(landlord of the pub when John first frequented it)*. I always called him Mr Salvidge. Jean's dad. He was in the First World War and he used to regale us with his stories with what happened in the trenches. There were a couple of old timers from the First World War.

Was there always a local WI?

Stella: I don't know about that, but we had a Mother's Union. I can remember going to that, I've got photos of the Mother's Union. Women's Institute? I haven't been a member very long but it goes back, I would say, it's got to have been going forty years, when did we move into the cottage down the road? No. 44… [in] 'sixty-three, yeah, so it's been going since the early nineteen-sixties in its present form. Like John said, there was a youth club; we had the village hall which had as part of it a management committee and a social committee, fundraising. I was secretary.

John: Loads of dances…

Stella: We had loads going on – fetes, skittles weekends until recently and as we've gotten older, a lot of us have given up. But then again, that was when all the farms were farms. Jowett family owned Lower West, Higher West and Manor [Farms]; the Yeomans owned Walk, Tynemead and Moorleaze, so of course there were loads of farmers and farm workers in the village. Now all the farms, more or less, have turned into houses and properties and what have you. Everybody else goes outside to work. There isn't work in the village so you haven't got…well, there is a nice community spirit, but there isn't a working community.

Kitty Cox (Stella's mother) with cat, outside no.42 after getting married in 1938

19

John: There's only five working herds in the village now. There's many cows though – bigger herds. You used to have fifty to a hundred, but now it's three hundred odd [per herd].

Stella: We had fancy dress at the pub. At harvest suppers and New Year's Eve dances we had hundred and twenty people. The commitee all did the work. We didn't buy anything in, we all did it.

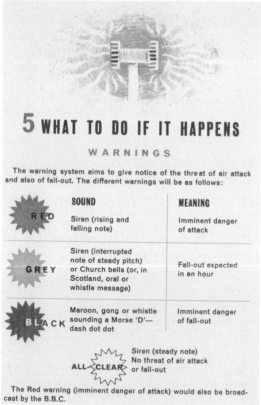

5 WHAT TO DO IF IT HAPPENS

WARNINGS

The warning system aims to give notice of the threat of air attack and also of fall-out. The different warnings will be as follows:

	SOUND	MEANING
RED	Siren (rising and falling note)	Imminent danger of attack
GREY	Siren (interrupted note of steady pitch) or Church bells (or, in Scotland, oral or whistle message)	Fall-out expected in an hour
BLACK	Maroon, gong or whistle sounding a Morse 'D'— dash dot dot	Imminent danger of fall-out
ALL-CLEAR	Siren (steady note) No threat of air attack or fall-out	

The Red warning (imminent danger of attack) would also be broadcast by the B.B.C.

Advising the householder on protection from nuclear attack, 1963

John: I like the way it is at the moment.

Stella: Yeah, it's getting back to what it used to be a bit.

John: We don't attend all the things we used to. We're getting on a bit now and family as well.

Stella: We don't like the noisy music! (*laughs*)

John: Did you hear about when I spoke to Michael [McGarvie] about the arrival of the nuclear age in Witham?

I'd love to find out where the village klaxon went…

John: It was worrying times, the sixties with the cold war. The early warning was absolutely useless.

Stella: It was no good to anybody; you wouldn't have even have gotten a helmet on, would you?

John: It was a four minute warning, that's all the time we had, just sitting under the table waiting for it to happen – would have been a complete waste of time. It wasn't just the threats between America and Russia, but all the bombs that could go off from the other big countries – France, China, Great Britain. Huge things they would have been.

Stella: And they moan about pollution now.

John: And worries about a chain reaction which would have been the end of the world, and it could have happened. That was the worrying thing when we were bringing up our two daughters. That's one thing I remember, and the klaxon. They [klaxons] must have gone to most villages then.

Do you remember the estate being sold up?

Stella: Yeah, some of the cottages…

Did that make a big difference to the village?

Stella: It must have done in the end, because, you know, the farms changed hands, and then they ended being up three or four farms together after it… farmers couldn't seem to, they just disappeared…like the Jowetts who bought three or four and the cottages were bought for…

John: …less than a hundred pound.

Stella: Well, Mr Smith bought his for forty or fifty pounds. I think it was fifty pounds…that was the end one up at Kerry Croft. At the end, nearest the two bungalows, all the cottages down in the yard, they were all sold, all of them, I mean – nearly the whole village [had] belonged to the Duke.

John: No facilities at all. When we moved into no. 44 there was a copper and a fire underneath…that we used to boil up to do the washing. You used it a couple of times, didn't you?

Stella: Oh, we had to.

John: We had to do the washing and when we moved out they put a bathroom in for us.

The farm did that?

John: Yeah, the Jowetts. We moved in with Stella's mum while they gutted it and put in a bath for us with an inside toilet and hot water.

Stella: It was nice to go to an inside toilet (*laughs*).

Arthur Cox (Stella's father) in his Home Guard uniform, outside no.42

Because the other thing was the allotments. They were next door to…

John: Well I had an allotment, I had two patches there. Years ago, where the bungalows are now, that used to be allotments right the way down through. Right the way to the Yard. There were allotments coming up that way, and all these cottages and allotments went that way, so it must have been two acres of allotments.

Stella: All belonged to the Duke again, you see. The cottages belonged to the Duke so everybody had allotments to grow your own.

John: Everybody there, you could see what they were all planting. I always remember your dad saying that he used to doff his hat if the Duke went through.

Stella: Oh they did…

John: I couldn't do that you see. I'd've been excommunicated – I wouldn't doff my cap.

During the water crisis, at the meetings when the Duke was there everybody else called him "Your Grace, your Grace," and I was thinking, I can't say it, I can't say it. *(laughs)*

John: Well if you were really rude to him in those days he could boot you out of your cottage. They had the power to do that – I don't know how I would have gotten on in those days…

Stella: YOU would have been in gaol.

John: They must have had some punch ups around the pubs years ago, with drunkards falling in the ditch. That's what lock ups were mainly for: drunk people that couldn't go home.

Herb Salvidge's cows in the yard outside the Seymour Arms, early nineteen-sixties

When we first moved down, a neighbour that lived in Nunney used to come here every Friday night because there was dancing in the village hall in Witham. He said that Friday night wasn't Friday night unless there was a punch up, as simple as that.

Stella: We've had a few punch-ups in the hall, I'm afraid. Outsiders…

He would have been an outsider; a boy from Nunney.

Stella: Oh Nunney… Nunney or Wanstrow.

John: Those were the days.

Stella: The good old days! *(laughs)*

John: Years ago when we had skittles alongside the pub, some undesirable from Frome was saying some indecent things apparently. Off he went up the road – I thought that I had better do something – so I thought I'd ring the police. I could get back to the skittles then, 'cos I was the organiser, like. When the police turned up and they asked for a description from me, they said it was very unusual to get a call from Witham because "You usually handle these things yourselves."

So there was a skittle alley in the barn?

John: No, we used to have a portable one alongside the pub.

Stella: Whether it really was a club room [building in the pub yard] years and years ago, I don't know. Presumably they used it [for the Friendly Society] but not that I can ever remember. It's always been as it is now, really.

The Seymour Arms was a farm as well?

Stella: Oh yeah, the cows were in the yard where the cars are parked now, and the men's toilets were opposite across the yard from the pub. The problem was that when strangers came in the pub and needed the toilet, they had to go through the cows to get to the men's toilet. If the ladies needed the toilet they would ask if they could use the upstairs loo, 'cos there was no ladies loo as such…

John: When the cows were in for the winter they'd stand in the yard ready for milking and one chap come in one day, quite posh, and he said "Excuse me, but could you tell me where the toilets are?" I said "Yeah, it's that door out through the gate" and he came back in through the front door almost cross-legged, saying "I can't find them" so I said I would show him. I went out the back door and opened the gate and said "There, look, in that tin shed." And he said "So have I got to walk through those beasts?"

Commemorative brick above the exterior door of the Seymour Arms toilet extension

Took him across and the cows just parted. They were all pets really.

Stella: Dead easy, Buttercup…

John: They all had names so I said I would take him through. The toilet had no roof and the slate to go against…there was no sit-down. You ought to have preserved it!

When were the indoor toilets put in?

John. The ones we have now? Well, I helped dig the foundations for those and Keith [Dicker] finished the topping off. It was a village job.

Did anybody get as far as Bath or Bristol?

Stella: Yes, my mum and dad had friends in Bristol and we used to catch the bus into town on the Saturday morning. We then caught the bus from Frome, the old green buses to Bristol which went every which way. We didn't stay for a day. You had to stay for a week because it took a day to get there and a day to get back, it's like going to Australia and New Zealand these days.

John: One chap died not that long ago and he'd never been further north than Bristol. His brother took him up the tarmac to Effingham and Les thought it was London, I won't say a surname (*laughs*) and that's the furthest he'd been…

Were there any church trips or school trips to the sea side?

Stella: We had one trip a year to the seaside on the train and the county provided our packed lunch for the children. We used to go on the train, and the church used to do day trips, only the odd one or two a year, and if I remember rightly, the pantomime at Bath or Bristol.

John: Pub outings…

Stella: Yeah, you had pub outings.

John: The Derby, and football, some show in Bristol, all blokes, bread and beer in the back of the bus, as men do…I mean to go to Epsom, years ago… the coach from Maiden Bradley!

Did you used to have those very upright leather seats that we used to have on our school bus? You would go around the corner and we all slid off.

Stella: We did to start with…you either had the leather type seats or the sort of fibre-y type seats.

John: They had some boneshakers too, cos when the lads used to go on the bus to Frome and there had been trouble, the bus would leave the car park in bottom gear to come up over Bath Street, the chaps had to walk alongside the bus, and they used to bash their fists [on the window] and one night we even had a brick come through the window on the bus!

Stella: They could go faster on their feet than the bus could go on wheels.

John: And it was a half-cab coach, with the driver sat on his own, and all the way up Bath Street the young lads would chase the coach. That's going back a long time…fifty years ago.

Stella: More than that. We had the papers delivered everyday by bike. Horace Allen delivered the papers to Witham, Gare Hill, all the way around.

From Frome?

Stella: No, he lived here.

John: There was a family of four or five that lived in a cottage next to the old smithy.

Stella: Three brothers and two sisters. But Horace delivered the papers, it used to take him all day, you used to get the news the next day really…

John: When I worked at Cary's all those years ago, we picked up the papers at half past four in the afternoon!

Stella & John running skittles in the Seymour Arms garden to raise funds for the History Project. August 24, 2014

Ronald Harding, Farmer, 96

Ron aged twelve in his Keyford College uniform, with his younger sister Clarice and elder sister Madge, 1928

I had my first date after the war, by which time I was getting on a bit. We courted for five years but I never felt like asking her to marry me. The spark just wasn't there. She liked horses, and what good is that?

Ron Harding was born when the battle of Verdun was raging on the Western Front. He lived at Bellerica for eighty-five of his ninety-six years, was married in 1960 and sold his eighty-strong dairy herd in 1973. When the time came to leave in 2007, he had spent barely a handful of days away from the parish. He moved to Highfield House Residential Home, in Castle Cary, where he made friends and enjoyed the most extraordinary and loving care to the last moments of his life. And so his last five years, like his first, were spent away from his beloved Bellerica.

I was born on 25th June 1916 at home in Longbridge Deverill. It was an olde worlde house built in timber style and I believe it is intact even to this day. I last visited in the 1980s. I've got only vague memories of the inside. Father rented the dairy and the cows: presumably the land and the house were thrown in for the rent. Father also employed men to help him.

Just three months before my fourth birthday we left Longbridge and moved to Bellerica on Lady Day, 25th March, 1920. We travelled the ten miles to our new home all together in a trap pulled by Tommy the horse, with a thick rug over our knees. I have sketchy memories of first casting eyes on Bellerica. It seemed a bit dark and gloomy in the beginning. It was an upheaval for mother and father to move; but it was a sad sight seeing father walking up through the orchard with his dog on the day, forty years later, that he moved out.

Money was short and when father came to Bellerica it was the first farm he had owned. He had bought it – the house, stone buildings, one hundred and sixty five & a half acres – in 1919 for £7,500 at an auction at the George Hotel in Frome, to which he had cycled from Longbridge Deverill. He took out a mortgage to buy it, but in the early twenties the prices of farms fell and a recession hit. The price of milk also fell and father often said then that he wished his bike had broken on the way to the auction!

I think I slept in what is now called the Tudor room, where the medieval fireplace was found. When I wasn't well I'd sleep in the spare room, where, when I was older, I learned to ride a fairy cycle. When we came to Bellerica there were the four bedrooms there are today, plus the cheeseroom, but no bathroom upstairs. One of the first things mother showed us was where the toilet was outside – there were no such facilities inside back then. She also took us into the dining room, which made quite an impression with its flagstones and oak timbered ceiling. It seemed dark to me, though, because it had a heavy lacquering on it. However, over the years it has been admired by many people and one suggestion was that it had been taken from the ceiling of a fighting ship similar to the Victory at Portsmouth. We spent most of our time there after we had first moved in. For years we had coconut matting on the floor. Mother took it up annually and threw tea leaves around on the stone floor, collecting them along with the dust.

They made cheese in the dairy, which was taken up to the 'play room' for storage and to mature. Big cheeses were nearly 100lbs each while the smaller ones, called truckles, were around 10lbs. When my sister Madge was about six and me four – so not long after moving into Bellerica – we both managed to contract whooping cough. Our coughs persisted for many months. Mother tried to build us up with cod liver oil and Vinol so when Auntie Amy and I were having tea at Uncle Archie's farm house at Toller near Dorchester she, referring to me, said: "He is not very strong." I was fuming underneath but could not say a word. However, in some ways since it has stood me in good stead because when Mary, my wife, asks me to do something I don't fancy doing I lightheartedly say: "I'm not very strong."

I was five when I started school at Upton Noble, in a section of what is now the village hall. What wasn't nice was the poverty of some of the children who attended school, their feet showing through their worn boots. Separating the two sides of the building was a huge green curtain. Miss Walter, who was a very kind lady, was my first teacher. I liked school but between lessons we had an hour and a half break, during which I would walk home for lunch.

I played a lot with Madge. [She] was two years older than me and really was my playmate. Together we made up a playroom in the attic, where we had a horse on wheels and a hobby horse. We were happy to go up in daylight, but too scared to go up the stairs in the dark (those were the days when we went round with candles and had paraffin lamps on the tables). Later I had a green wooden engine which I pushed around. It had iron wheels which rattled all through the dairy over its flagstones. My other sister Clarice was ten years younger and born at Bellerica. I was more grown up by this time and she wasn't such a playmate to me. She used to like combing father's hair, but when she got tired of that she would give him a bang with the brush.

We were given a few pennies for pocket money, which we would spend on sweets in the shop at the bottom of the churchyard in Upton Noble, run by a Mrs Austin. She never weighed them for a penn'orth and she always said they were pure boiled sweets. There wasn't much money to go around in those days, but Mrs Austin was always generous and you got a whole bag of sweets for 1d. She sold cheese, too, plus other groceries and I remember everywhere being very clean. You walked through the front door and into a parlour, while on the left was their dining room. Her brother was a wheelwright and he took days to make one wheel. I took in the process each time I bought sweets.

I remember around the time that I was five and Madge seven, father liked a duck egg for breakfast. We had about eight ducks which swam in the pond in the orchard and waddled in to their little house near Bellerica back door for their evening feed and so they were safe from the fox. The pond around which Madge and I used to spend many hours sailing toy boats was about one hundred and fifty yards from the kitchen window. Mother liked to keep an eye on us from there, although her view was partly obscured by the garden wall. One lovely day when the pond had shrunk a little, due to a dry summer, I had to walk in to the dried area to reach the water when I tripped over a stone and fell into about two feet of water, almost in the middle of the pond. I must have swallowed a fair amount because I was in a state of shock and I managed to cough up a large amount of the brown stuff that the ducks had paddled in. Our next concern, rather than my recovery, was how to avoid mother knowing what had happened. The solution was for me to completely strip off all my wet clothes and hang them on the hedge, which we did for a couple of hours. Our plan worked and our idyllic play area was assured.

I've got no recollection of our early holidays, but when I was about seven or eight I do remember going to Weymouth. We caught the train at Witham Friary. You sometimes had to stand as the trains were so packed. It stopped at every station and we learned all the names by heart as trips here became fairly frequent. It is where my love of the sea began. The station was in the middle of the town, but the beach was a comfortable walk away. I remember having many rides on donkeys at Weymouth, while another regular haunt was Grimstone, near Dorchester, where Archie, one of mother's brothers, and his wife, Annie, lived. In 1925 Archie drove to Bellerica in his new car, a Citroen 10, and I remember riding back to his home in it.

Madge and I went to Shepton Mallet to have our tonsils out – we were very young at the time. I was nine and she was eleven. I remember the mask being placed over my face. I can still see it coming towards me; the shape of it and everything. One nurse held my legs and the other my arms but I was resigned to it and didn't struggle. When they took the mask towards Madge, though, she did make a fuss. But it was the norm in those days – nip the tonsils if they were big.

At eleven I started at Keyford College in Frome. It is now no more. Getting to school involved cycling to Witham, taking the train to Frome – they were steam then, had closed carriages and I used a season ticket – and walking from Frome station up Locks Hill about a mile to Keyford, which was a private school. The worst thing was the journey home, especially in the winter, which involved an uphill bicycle ride in the dark. I used an acetylene lamp, with carbide in the bottom, which combined to give a good light. Sometimes, though, it ran out and I would cycle along in the dark. I was frightened at times but generally there weren't the problems that you hear about these days.

The day I was due to buy the aforementioned bike I awoke to find spots on my chest and I knew that I had caught chicken pox. I was so keen, however, to choose this bike that I kept my secret and went to Halfords in Frome where father purchased one for £4/12/6. We put it in the guards' quarters on the train to Witham and I rode it the two miles home. However, at the half way stage on the steep hump-back bridge over the railway I had to dismount as the effect of my complaint was taking its toll. Another day while riding to the station outside Binden Cottage (now the Crouches' farm [Grazemoor]) a large spaniel ran out, which I hit, flying over the handlebars. I damaged my bike and had to go home again. All that cycling certainly kept me fit and for years, to save time in the mornings, I would jog to get the cows in, often to the far side of the farm. What put paid to all that was having my first hip operation in the early 1980s. You can't run a step after that – ever.

If father hadn't paid for my schooling I could have stayed at Upton Noble until the end. The standard of my education improved once I had moved to Keyford College, where there was a far greater choice of subjects, including French and a choice of Latin or Euclid, which turned out to be a difficult form of geometry invented two thousand years before. I thought I knew quite a bit of French until I heard two nuns talking on Frome station one day – I couldn't understand a word they were saying. We were given lots of homework, which was sometimes neglected as I didn't get home until six-thirty. I enjoyed English grammar best of all and in those days was good at it. We were given mental arithmetic tests and had to shout out the answers. I took no exams but was preparing for an Oxford exam – Oxford Juniors and Oxford seniors were the equivalent of today's GCSEs – when the school closed down, mainly due to a lack of pupils. I was sixteen and I never went back to education. In those days it was expected that you would go into your family business. There really weren't the opportunities then to go on to further education.

The pre-war years were difficult for my father. He had trouble finding decent workers for the farm until Dick Loxton came, who was a friend of the family. He worked at Bellerica for five years and then started working for Uncle Gilbert at Manor Farm. I worked on the farm at weekends while I was still at school, usually milking the cows by hand. I was generally given the easy ones to do. When I left school I did general farm work, carrying on with the milking and doing the horses occasionally if the farm worker was away. I ploughed the ten acre field with a horse once.

I also fed the cattle, mucked out the stalls, made ricks in the fields during the summer and for the winter feed cut the hay into squares (trusses) and loaded them on to the wagon on our heads. That then had to be offloaded into the cow stall. There were, of course, no balers in those days. If we had a bad summer we would still be hay making in September. Half of the fields were used for hay and half for grazing.

In the early days we had around forty cows with fifteen youngsters for replacement. We went to the Wednesday market at Frome with the calves who would be transported on a float, tied down with a rope or under netting. I don't know how the cows were taken to market back then but by the 1930s they were starting to be transported by lorry.

I was paid thirty shillings a week, with board and lodgings all in – a form of pocket money really. The hours were long. I would get up at five-thirty and fetch the cows in from the field. At six pm the day would usually be over, when I would go in to tea, except during haymaking, when the work would go on into the darkness.

If I wanted to go out I would borrow father's car. In fact, I didn't get my own until after I was married in 1960. My parents got their first car in 1930 – Uncle Archie's old Citroen. You never bought new. Archie replaced it with a nice Hillman saloon. The Citroen was stolen in Frome. We had parked in Badcox and gone off to do some shopping and when we came back it was gone. It was a shock and totally unexpected as things like that didn't tend to happen then. But there were no keys, just a press button starter, so it was easy for anyone to drive away. It was found in Bath and we had to go and fetch it. The brakes had been damaged but otherwise it was intact.

By 1933 I had reached the age of seventeen. Madge and I decided to apply for a driving test after both of us had spent many sessions practicing with L plates, both together and Madge sometimes with her boyfriend. You had to learn to 'double-declutch' when changing down. There were no synchromesh gears in those days and it needed lots of practice to achieve perfection. I put the hood down on the Citroen and we set off on a lovely day to negotiate the forty miles to Taunton, the longest drive I had taken, both full of confidence. We duly arrived at a posh house in the town and were met by a genial gent (an ex-army officer I reckon). He passed us both saying to Madge: "Your brother has had more driving experience but you answered more Highway Code questions." The folk at home expressed surprise at our success. What a cheek!

As we grew up a lot of our friends had parties, including friends at Witham. On Christmas day we often went to Horsehill Farm at Evercreech, where father's father, James Harding, lived. I think we went there more often than we stayed at home, going by trap in the early days and then hiring a car. I also liked going to dances and whist drives in the local villages and hunt balls in Frome which were really popular. I really don't know where I got the energy from. I think the dances were probably my favourite entertainment, although I could have done with ballroom lessons. When I was seventeen I had lessons in formation dancing at Witham throughout one winter. I think part of the reason was that I liked Miss Ayres, the girl who ran the class and who came from Frome. Her mother was the musical director of the amateur dramatics shows. She was keen on me – if she had to demonstrate a move she would come up to me – but at the end of the last session I wished her goodbye and that was the end of that. She was two years older then me but it was my fault that I never heard from her again.

When Chamberlain went to Berlin to sign the 'peace' deal in 1938 we had just bought our first radio, a compact set called a Cossor, which was portable and involved a man coming round with an accumulator every week to recharge the battery. Clarice was in hospital having a kidney operation that year and we were worried about the bombing starting, but then we heard Chamberlain's promise of peace and for a while felt relieved. Of course it was an empty promise. On that Cossor we also heard Churchill's 'No Surrender' speeches in 1940 that inspired the nation.

I registered to join the army in 1940 when I was twenty three but I was given an exemption because of my occupation. If I had wanted to go and fight I could have done but how could I walk out on the farm? Food production was vital. I joined the Home Guard after an appeal was made by Anthony Eden, the foreign secretary, after the collapse of France. Everyone had to do something. You were enrolled and the first training session took place at the Seymour Arms, the pub at Witham Friary, in the spacious loft [clubroom] above the pub [outbuildings].

We used our own shotguns from the farm in the early days, although these had to be checked and passed for use. The sergeant instructors came from the camp at Marston near Frome but one day one came from the Welsh Guards. He told us that he'd had a bad experience at Dunkirk and commented: "HE is coming here and nothing's going to stop him. When those divebombers come overhead it is terrifying." That was defeatist talk and he never came again. I was in the Home Guard for the duration of the war, the last three years transferring to Wanstrow hall for training sessions. We made ourselves a firing range at Nunney and practised throwing real bombs. We always shot real bullets, including those in the school yard at Mrs Nicholls' house.

Early in the war we went on patrol one or two nights a week near Witham, on the lookout for German paratroopers. We heard our first bombs go off in Asham Wood near Nunney – maybe ditching on their way back to Germany. In the early days we all thought that *they* had come. My closest encounter with the Germans occurred in 1940 – on 25th September to be precise. I was ploughing and there had been a big raid on Filton Aerodrome with over a hundred killed. Every single plane from that raid flew over me on my tractor in Plough Field. You could see the black crosses on the planes. I got off the tractor, ran out of Plough Field and got down to the relative shelter of the road. I also saw a couple of Spitfires, but they were powerless to do anything against what was a force of around one hundred planes. The sky was just black with them. One Sunday night in early 1941 there was a big raid on Bristol and we could hear the planes, guided all the time by the search lights. We could also see flashes of explosions. *(German aircrews observed the fires burning at Bristol from a distance of 150 to 170 kilometres.)* In contrast to that terrible raid on Filton, two years later when the Russians had turned the tables on the Germans I was standing in the same field when I saw a mighty force of American Flying Fortresses with fighter escort flying westwards in groups of fifty. They were on their way to bomb the submarine pens at Brest.

Later in the war, when I was in Plough Field haymaking, I saw a Dornier bomber being attacked by two Spitfires. It had followed the railway line up from Frome and was flying low and they couldn't seem to hit it. It veered off and went up the hill towards Stourton, after which I saw a plume of smoke rising. You didn't read about such things in those days but it had obviously crashed. At that late stage, though, we all wondered why a plane had strayed so far inland.

Also late in the war I was in the Tudor room during a thunderstorm when a twin-engined Anson bomber flew round at a very low altitude with the tip of his wing burnt away – he had been struck. He made an emergency landing in Marlpit thirty acres field – I could see the dirt flying up – at which point I ran out of the house and sprinted all the way up to the field. I was greeted with the sight of five RAF men who had just alighted from the plane. They asked where the nearest pub was and set off for The Lamb. The plane was a virtual write-off and it took ages to get it removed from the field. A lot of people came to take a look. In fact we used to see a lot of planes flying over. There was an airfield at Gasper near Mere. Father even made a stretcher as a contingency plan but thankfully it was never used.

They got the odd bomb over Batcombe and we often wondered if someone had shown a light. The Germans dropped foil on the land to confuse the radar. Once I picked up two bundles that had not been untied.

We were all required to fit blackout curtains to all windows – although we had no electric during the war; that wasn't installed until afterwards. You just had to poke around in the dark, even with the cows.

We heard about the end of the war on the radio. I ended the war with a rifle, a Sten gun and one stripe. There were fantastic celebrations around the country when peace was declared. I do not remember taking part in any – I expect we all went to church – except the 'winding up' of the Home Guard at Batcombe. We had a meal in the village hall and Ted Arney, who captained our platoon at Wanstrow so amicably, gave a speech thanking us for our co-operation, even when a few swear words were directed at us. Our final cricket match was played at Upton Noble against Brewham who had not lost a match that season. It fell to me to make the winner with a boundary four. A delighted Ted told me: "That four was worth a hundred."

I had my first date with Peggy Maclean. It was after the war, by which time I was getting on a bit. I met her as my mother was friendly with hers and we used to visit them near Bristol. Even before we had a car her father would come and fetch us. She was eight years younger than me and we courted for five years but I never felt like asking her to marry me. When the novelty wore off I called it a day. The spark just wasn't there. She liked horses, and what good is that?

I met [my future wife] Mary in Yeovil when I was introduced by Aunt Trix, mother's sister. Mary had a flat and Trix lived nearby. She told Mary that she had a nephew she wanted her to meet and one night she took me round to see Mary. We knocked on the door and I can still remember her walking down the stairs. Trix was almost blind – she had been hit by a car a few years earlier. It was 1958; I was just over forty and Mary was thirty three. I had wasted the five previous years going up to Bristol. At the time Mary was working at Westlands and whenever she had a trip this way she would make a detour.

The evening of that first meeting I was invited to a dance with Mary and her Westlands friend Edith. It was something I liked anyway. Afterwards I would travel to Yeovil once a week following milking and have a meal with Mary. After a couple of years we were invited to stay at Teignmouth and my plan was to propose but Mary's sister Margaret and her husband Basil turned up out of the blue and scuppered all my plans. It was several months before I plucked up the courage again, on an evening in Mary's flat in front of a roaring fire. I decided to come out with it in plain English without going down on my knees, saying:

"Will you marry me?"

She said: "Oh yes." And that was that.

We began planning a September wedding in which I had no say, although that didn't bother me much – while mother and father got cracking getting Orchard Villa, their new home, built.

We went to Bath to buy the engagement ring and to Yeovil to get the wedding ring, along with six teaspoons which have now gone mildewed. After an engagement of around seven months we tied the knot on 19th September 1960. Mary was thirty-five and I was forty-four. The ceremony took place at St James Church in Teignmouth. We drove away in our Rover 75, headed for our honeymoon in Widemouth Bay near Bude in Cornwall. I had planned for a week but mother persuaded me to take a fortnight off – probably the longest I was ever away from the cows. Part of the honeymoon was also spent at Teignmouth, and it rained for evermore. We still have hundreds of the presents we were given, not least a pretty spotted tea set from Madge, a dinner service from Clarice and a Teasmaid, our gift from Westlands.

I took over the farm from 1960 onwards when I got married and mother and father moved up to Orchard Villa. Father still helped, well into old age, doing things like feeding the calves. The transition worked well and I enjoyed running the farm on my own.

1972 was a sad year for Mary and me. Father died of a heart attack in May that year; Mary's mother, Kathleen Goodenough, of angina at Bellerica and Madge in September of cancer. We were saddened by these losses and the following year I decided to take a break from dairying and to sell the cattle and most of the machines and then to sell the grass feed. The cattle sale was held on April 1st 1973, the morning of which was the windiest and stormiest one could imagine. One employee, John Singer, was away ill and I only had Otto Diener to assist. I got up at four a.m. only to find the tractor suffering from a flat large tyre. Obliging tyre people from Evercreech solved that problem, the weather improved and Mr Quick [the Cooper & Tanner auctioneer] conducted the sale which probably showed a deficit of £1,000 due to the weather. The grass feed sale was held later.

Was it a fulfilling life? It was on the whole. I liked being my own boss but if you stay at home you have to agree with your father. Everyone has their ups and downs.

Ron Harding flanked by his father, Graham (left); Otto Diener, a former POW (right); and John Singer (behind). Bellerica, late nineteen-fifties

Roy Wheeler, 82

The POWs made me a draughts board one Christmas; I wish I still have it but it got lost in time like everything does.

I was born on 23rd October 1932 at Binden Cottage in Witham Friary, which is two miles up on the Upton Noble side. At the age of five I went to Witham school until the age of eleven, and after that I went by train to Shepton school until the age of fifteen although I could have left at fourteen. I stayed on an extra year. I've got a sister and a brother. Sister lives in Frome and brother lives down Yeovil. Basically that's it.

What are your earliest memories?

My earliest are of when I was about three years old. At Christmas you usually had an orange, an apple, a few nuts and that was it. Maybe a little book or something. Except for that once when they treated me to the metal pedal car. They must've really saved up for that because there was never any money about in those days. I can remember tearing around the house in it. I suppose mainly playing around the house because we had a very big garden in which you could run around. From about the age of five onwards, even in those days you could do little odd jobs around the Jackson's farm at Great West, fetching and carrying little things, things you could carry around. Cos right from the age of eleven I could use horses, you know, these Shire horses.

Every year a steam traction engine would visit the farms, hauling a threshing machine, a water bowser and a caravan, to thresh wheat, barley and oats. At this time of year the farmers used to help one another. Mr & Mrs Stevens and their daughter farmed at Little West Barn which was over the other side of the railway from where I lived and I can remember helping helping them as well as the Jacksons. Another thing I can remember – when I was about eight or nine, during the school holidays we used to go across the fields right down to the Shepton Mallet line which is a good half to three quarters of a mile [walk]. We used to build dens there by the river. In those days it didn't matter, you could stay away all day and nobody worried. We had some friends, Arthur and Derek White who lived in the cottage about a mile down the road. We used to play with them a lot, up to the age of eleven when I went to Shepton [school]. I caught the train about twenty past eight I think it was. I cycled down from Binden Cottage. My Nan lived at no. 17 up the rank which was the other side of the line, and I left my bike there.

Were children that age expected to work and help?

You did automatically because it was during the war. Everybody mucked in.

Your first memories of war?

Rations is the first thing that comes to mind. I think we had to go into Frome to get coupon books in the first place. One for clothing, there was one for all the different foods, like cheese, butter, meat, bread – all sorts of things. Out where we were we weren't short of anything. We kept chickens for eggs and meat, you could get wild rabbit, we had a great big garden there and we grew everything. Apples and things like that. Plenty of orchards around. Fruit, pears, plums. The fields around Binden Cottage used to be covered in mushrooms. The farm across the other side the railway, they had a walnut tree and that used to fruit every year, so Christmas we had walnuts and hazelnuts. In those days you could go out and pick them. And another thing during the war – we used to pick rosehips. It's like a rosebush with a berry on it. They make rosehip syrup. Yes, we used to get paid so much a pound for it.

You only had so much butter and stuff but we were lucky because we worked on the farm. They made butter and cheese and they killed sheep, pigs and cows illegally.

Illegally?

Illegally because they weren't supposed to; everything were to go in the food chain, [but] it didn't. Even the police inspector and superintendent used to come out and get their share. I remember on more than one occasion when driving underage on the roads the inspector and I used to wave to one another as he realised I could get him into a lot of trouble!

At school I can remember the German bombers coming over in 1940 & '41, because we were on the flight path for Bristol. When they came over we were pushed into the smaller room [in the school] against the wall where the windows were all wire-meshed over and we had to wait until they had gone over. I saw dogfights in the sky when we were allowed out. They dropped any bombs they had left when the fighters were after them. Out where I lived out on the Brewham road there used to be a small signal box and they dropped a bomb near there one night. I don't think they were after that. They were after the railway. They never hit it, the railway anywhere along here. Which was surprising; you would have thought they would have really gone for it.

Then, after Dunkirk, the British tanks used to stop outside the school and brew up tea, stuff like that. Very often you would see them out there. It was mainly British tanks because they were smaller than the American ones. They would come all up around past us up to Upton Noble on manoeuvres.

Did prisoners of war work in Witham?

On Great West Barn farm where my dad worked for Mr Jackson there was two; one was a pilot and the other an infantryman. They worked on the farm and they were brought in from the prisoner of war camp opposite Frome College and taken back everyday. One Christmas they were allowed out if anybody would have them. Mum and dad had the two that worked on the farm and they made a draughts board for me, polished it up somehow. I wish I still had it but it got lost in time like everything else. The POWs were very friendly, very friendly indeed, and good workers...

Could they speak English?

Very good English, actually. Probably better than we did. They never tried to escape...stayed until the end of the war and were gradually repatriated back. After the war mum and dad kept in touch with the pilot and actually went over to Germany two or three times. Dad worked on the railway then and they could go all the way free on the train.

Land girls worked on the farm too. They were stationed somewhere around Frome but I'm not sure where, they were bussed out everyday as well…and mum did, during the summer months when they were really busy, mum did as well.

What do you remember of the Land Girls?

They were very flirty, I remember that. As a matter of fact, two of those got married around here, one in Witham – I won't say who because the family is still about – and the other one at Upton Noble.

Do you have any memories of the Home Guard?

Yes, my dad was a member of the Home Guard. He was a Sergeant and he had a Browning machine gun, which he kept at home. They went out at night when there were bombing raids on in case any planes were shot down so they could capture the crew. That was basically the reason. Although they were trained in proper warfare in case as they thought in the early part of the war the Germans were coming over.

I remember you telling me a story about the American soldiers…

It was down by the pub and the black Americans and the white Americans didn't get on, which was stupid but they never did. The black Americans were down at Witham pub along with some Green Howards – some white Americans came down and started picking on the black Americans and the Green Howards told them to lay off and of course they didn't. They thought we treated them the same as they did – so the Green Howards just pitched into them, and they really did pitch into them!

Somebody must have called the American MPs because they came out and the Green Howards said: "If you touch the black Yanks you'll get the same as the others did." They didn't cos the Green Howards were stationed at Marston Park, and the Americans were as well. After that they only allowed the black Yanks in a couple of days a week and whites another two days a week [to keep separate].

Was it mostly beer served at the Seymour Arms in the war?

Yes. There were two breweries in Frome in those days. I don't think they served so much cider in those days because all the farms made their own. You could go to almost any farm and they would make cider. I don't think the soldiers could've stood the cider.

Did you talk to the American soldiers?

Quite a few…they were alright, because they always had chocolate and sweets. They were after the girls…two in Witham that I could remember although I was only about ten. There was one who, um, got one of the girls in trouble, but she was lucky. One of the locals took pity on her and married her, as a matter of fact they both died about a couple of years ago in Frome. They stayed together. The other one, she used to fly around with an American officer in a Jeep, I can remember that plainly. Gosh, she thought he was gonna marry her after the war – but no chance. She was lucky, another of the police boys married her and they lived in Frome.

How did the village feel with the troops all gone after D-Day?

It felt really dead. We were lucky as a village because in those days we had the trains and we used to go to Weymouth a lot. You could have a good day out in Weymouth. Quite cheap on the train. Especially Sundays. That station used to be packed!

So was that during the war, to get away?

Yes, it was for a day out. You couldn't do it all the time. Not during the war because troops and all that kind of thing had priority. A lot of people didn't realise that there was an aircraft factory in Frome. Down by where Butler and Tanner's is. They didn't make the whole ['plane]. I think they made parts for Halifax bombers. Because it was right on the railway – handy for the trains to take the parts for assembly elsewhere.

Were any young men from the village conscripted into the forces?

I only know of one – my uncle, Hubert Wheeler. He lived with grandmother and went into the infantry. Then he was a dispatch rider. In France after D-Day he got sent up to the front line with a message. He was told that the Americans would be at the crossroads but when he got there… no Americans. So he turned right and got about a hundred yards down the road and there was a German machine gun: he said he never turned a motorbike around so fast in his life!

He also was one of the first ones into Belsen Concentration camp. He would never talk about that. Not until the very end just before he died. He had a few words but other than that, no. I think it was too painful what they saw.

When did you go on National Service?

I was called up in February 1951. I did my initial training at Aldershot and then we moved to Blackdown, on the hills. Then I moved into Feltham in a transit camp and we were there for about three months while we were waiting for our postings. Eventually my posting came through to Benghazi in October 1951. I was lucky because I had about three weeks of Malta on the way out. We flew on from there to Benghazi. Between England and Malta we had several airlines but from Malta on to Benghazi we had

RAF Dakotas and you could see the daylight through the doors and they couldn't go above a certain height. They would rattle and shake but they got you there.

What can you remember about the city of Benghazi?

Roy during National Service

It was still rubble from the war basically, it was still a mess. Right in the harbour opening there was a munitions ship which sunk and they were afraid to move it in case it went [up]. We had our own fire service which was a Bedford van and a pump behind and we used to go down to the sea front to practice, I can remember the first time I got a hold of the hose, full power, and I nearly went into the sea. If you were good at sports in the army you got away with blue murder. I was lucky: I did football and running so every morning I'd go out at about four o'clock and did about twelve or fifteen miles which was just around the camp because it wasn't safe to go too far and I would come in after the others had their breakfast. And then we had a football match against the Arabs which was just over the border in Egypt. We were picked to play what was the proper Egyptian team, and we got there and changed and came out on the pitch and I couldn't believe my eyes! About every three or five feet was an armed Egyptian soldier. Apparently they were protecting us from the Arabs because at that time relations were terrible. I must admit that we were scared and made sure we didn't win. We drew, but we didn't win.

In the desert out there we had a munitions dump, a big one which was there from the war and about every three months it was our turn to go out there on guard duty. There's only three of you out there, a corporal and two privates – I was the corporal. We were at this ammunitions dump which was just a fenced-in place and heard this terrible noise. We thought "Oh crumbs, what's this?" It was about a thousand Arabs coming over the desert… But they weren't interested in us, they went on into Benghazi and I can tell you I was really scared because anything thrown in there [the dump] and the whole lot would have went… all the tank ammunition, the rifle and Sten gun ammo, grenades and heavy shells.

Just you and two privates…

Yeah, that's all they sent out there every night to guard it. And yet it was never touched.

Were you sorry to leave?

Uh, no. But that's when I made the biggest mistake of my life, I was offered to re-sign on when I came out and I said "No." They even offered to keep me as a corporal which they didn't usually do, because if you re-signed on you went back to [being a] private again. I said no, and about two or three years after I thought, "you silly clot!" I would have been out at forty-odd with a good pension but you don't think of these things at the time, do you?

What was the best thing about National Service?

Discipline. When you were told to do something you did it. I suppose you knew that when you were told to do something, you didn't have a choice. If you didn't do it you were in trouble. I think nowadays that would probably do a lot of youngsters good. I remember a few weeks after I was demobbed being in Witham pub with a few mates and I was talking to some of the farmers about all the running and sport I did in the Army and they bet me if I could do a mile in under four and a half minutes they would buy drinks all round. I did it in four minutes, twenty five seconds – drinks all round!

One of the harshest winters was '47.

I remember '47, it rained and froze at the same time, the roads and even the fields were ice. The following morning dad and I went up Witham to take the cows in for milking and into the sheds, well, you had a job to stand up even in the fields, and the cows as they walked along jingled!

Roy Wheeler on his 82nd birthday at the village hall, Witham Friary

Jingled?

From the icicles. But, even in those days the trains kept running because each section had a gang of workers and they kept their section free so the trains did keep running. As for trying to drive anywhere – it was almost impossible. The farmers were more lucky, the tractors could get around and you could get from one to another through the fields and get around it that way.

And then in '63 there was very heavy snow.

That started Boxing Day 1962. Thirteen foot drifts. Witham and Batcombe was completely cut off. At the station, the snow was level across from platform to platform. An engine with a snowplough soon cleared the station but during that winter my father, who worked at Blatchbridge signal box walked to work along the railway line to arrive there at six for early shift and left at midnight after late shift. The Thursday after Boxing Day, several of us dug one road out through towards Frome. The next night it all blew in again, so after that the farmers drove their tractors over the top, which you wouldn't think was possible but it was! You'd think it would go down but it was so compacted that it didn't. Everybody could just drive over the top. I came out every week because I was doing paraffin and every Monday I drove in and out…right through until late March.

Sorry, what were you doing?

Paraffin. It's what you used to use for lights, stoves and heating. One of my first jobs when I started from school was for Miller's Hardware in Frome. We used to go around all the villages with paraffin, and then we built a special van and it was like a shop for paraffin.

People must have been fed up with it by then.

They were, and the good thing about Witham was that we still had the trains; during this big freeze the farmers brought their stock to the station from where it was transported into Frome. The younger people went two or three times a week and brought bread and stuff back for the older people. That's the only way you would survive: community spirit; in those days everybody knew everybody. They lived their whole lives in the village.

After Mum left the village in 1981 I never came back until the fete last year and realised how fond I was of the village. When I saw you where doing a project on the last hundred years of the village, I thought "What a brilliant idea."

I am sure there are more memories in there somewhere…

Mavis Walker, 84

It was a very much an old country village; it had small tractors and a post office-cum-shop which sold just about everything, including the most delicious ham.

Mavis in her front garden picking off dandelion heads, April 13th, 2015

Mavis grew up in Chapel-en-le-Frith, part of a long established Buxton family. Her father was a farmer who discouraged his daughters to farm, so first she studied architecture in Manchester before market gardening and farming in Lincolnshire. Having met her future husband, a Buxton man, they got married in Ceylon and lived in India for twelve years as he was a tea planter. After a spell in Uganda they lived in Kenya for a further twenty years before returning to Buxton and retiring to Witham in September 1982.

Could you tell me when and why you came to Witham Friary?

We came here because we retired from Kenya in 1981. We had both come from Buxton, and we decided it was just too cold in winter to stay there. I came down and my husband said "Anywhere between Gloucester and the Devon border, I don't mind where you go." So I did. I had a sister-in-law down here, near Ilminster – we looked at dozens of houses, but I didn't want anything too modern. I wanted something old.

By sheer chance I had a load of cuttings; I saw this house and thought I would look at it, and I thought "Yes, this is a nice small village" – not spoilt, nice old houses, nice countryside, so I decided that I would look into it a bit more. I came back a bit later with my sister-in-law who looked at it, there were lots of problems but I phoned my husband and he said that if I liked it I should put buy it, so I put an offer in for it. I looked at three or four more in the area, as far as Gloucester, on my way back. My husband said that the estate agent had called and our offer had been accepted, and so we then put into motion selling our house [in Buxton]. My husband never even came to look at the house – we moved down within eight weeks and settled in quite quickly. It was a very different village to what it is now – it was very much an old country village, not with big tractors; it had small tractors and a post office-cum-shop which sold just about everything, including the most delicious ham.

Had the school already closed down?

The school had closed. When I first came [here] it was the village hall. The village hall has always done quite a lot – various people have taken it on and done various bits of redecorating and building work, and we still get quite a few functions there, a very handy place to have. We changed vicars two or three times…

Yes – when we first came here there was no vicar; we went to a carol service the first Christmas we were here.

How long have you been here?

Three years.

That was when he left…

We thought there was something missing from the service and figured out that it was the vicar.

Well, when we first came here there was no vicar. Then we had a vicar called Pescod who ran five parishes, he was here for a number of years before he moved on. I haven't heard any news of him recently. We were without a vicar for a while before we had the Reverend John Hodder, he was here quite a long time. He must have been here twenty years I should think, you would have to ask somebody in the church. He was here for a long time and of course then we were without a vicar again. That was very difficult because they were going to make three parishes into two – unfortunately they thought two vicars were retiring at the same, but they didn't, one stayed on so now one poor vicar is running eight parishes.

Were there more church services when you came here?

There was one every Sunday because we had a vicar, there were also one or two lay people who did them.

So now there's only one a month?

Yes, once a month. We do like to have a few more in between if we can. Sometime we get another vicar in if there's a special occasion because the present one is run off of his feet. He's married – it's too much even though he's a younger man – no older man could possibly do it. They did have a big kind of centenary at the church, I can't remember when it was but it was in about 1980, they had a big festival at the church. You should have some photos because I know they opened up the roof and John Hill had a ladder and I remember climbing into the roof of the church. It was very interesting and a terrific festival. I was working at the time and I can't remember any of the details – I was the treasurer at the time and I remember taking in a lot of money – somebody will remember.

Who ran the shop?

Peter Coombes, who I used to meet when I took the dog out – I often used to meet him and he used to show me different walks. After about two or three months he was suddenly knocking on my door saying: "I've got a proposition. I need somebody to come and work in the shop during the mornings for three mornings a week, while I go and collect bread and do the deliveries – would you be interested?"

I said "Yes" and then went to work at the post office for the next three years – I used to work Tuesdays and Thursdays and Saturdays. Peter did a lot for the village; he used to organise the fete which was held every year in the playground. He ran it very efficiently, and after a while he suggested that I be the treasurer and had me count out the money. I used to come home with lines of pennies and every imaginable coin. Before the village fete each year all the farmers and villagers would join in and clean it from one end to the other, and no weeds were seen – it was all tidied up and swept. It was beautiful. Everybody helped. Nearly every year the Duke of Somerset would come and open the fete with his children. It was very much a community. Three years later Peter left, other people moved in and took the post office over, but I continued to work there.

Meanwhile, all of the farms and things – because there was a big area which belonged to this one owner, the Jowetts – they sold it and it was split up and a new house was built up past the church, and that was made into a little farm. Larger tractors came in and more mess came with it! The big house which had been the manor house was split into two and the farmyards were opened up – what had been farmyards became two houses and where the calf and cow pens had been below the road – next to the playground – somebody bought that and built a house there. So the village began to grow quite a lot. Later, in the mid-nineties, houses were built on the other side of the bridge – New Friary Cottages. The quarry people, the Yeomans, sold that land and houses were built there. Behind there was the football field and that was lost – that changed hands, and again that then stopped. The village then managed to get the grounds opposite the Seymour Arms and made that into a football pitch. They were able to use that as their playground and children were allowed to play there.

You said you worked at Longleat.

After the shop closed I had a job delivering the papers, because the Stradlings took over the paper round. I delivered the papers to Horningsham and as far as Maiden Bradley, up to Gare Hill and back around through the village which took up to three hours. I did that for a number of years. The Stradling daughter went away for a while and when she came back she took it on, so I then got a job at Longleat working in the main shop in the house – where I stayed for sixteen years.

The Seymour Arms is run by the same people?

Yes. I think it was originally [run] by Jean's parents.

The Salvidges go back to the 1880s.

There was somebody called Caiger or somebody who had a farm near here somewhere; I don't know if you know them. Do you know anybody up at Gare Hill? The Proctors? Ron Proctor would be able to tell you more about that. He knows a lot because he came here as a boy – he was evacuated to the cottage across there *(gestures to No. 28)* all the way from London. He's got lots of stories about how the village was in the old days. It has changed a lot.

Has it? It doesn't look like it has changed at all in years and years.

Well before I first came, before all the food laws came in, at the pub she used to do very nice cold ham and salad lunches, they were very popular. She did those for years and a lot of the people who worked used to come especially to have this cold lunch. The new food laws came in and she needed three sinks and no way were they going to go into that – that stopped the food. It's a real shame.

It was a completely different village, of course not so many cars and there used to be a bus for workers which went to Frome in the morning – it was probably the school bus. Ruth Norman used to work in Frome at Minty's: she used to work there and go in on the bus every morning and come back every afternoon. That was stopped and we only have one a week now. It isn't much use. It doesn't get here until quarter past ten and then comes back at half past twelve. So it's very difficult for anybody who hasn't got a car.

The dovecot was…

That was lent out to anybody who would rent it. There was a lady who did photography and she used to have her studio there, she came two or three times a week, doing her work there. It was quite a long time before it was altered. Of course now you can see it, which is lovely. It has beautiful windows, the ones before had been broken by children throwing stones.

Grade 2* listed – a very important building.

I read some history of Witham the other day; it was originally intended as a guest house for the monastery.

I think that's about it. That's the end of the interview with Mavis Walker.

Geoff Sheppard, Farmer, 62

As far as I'm concerned I will never retire. I say to people, I'll just fade away. That's how I look at it.

Geoff is one of few people who can claim to have lived not just in the same village, but in the same house, for his entire life. A third generation farmer, he is still on the farming ladder started off by his grandfather as a smallholder in Chilcompton, near Radstock. He married Ann in 1977 and has now handed over the day to day running of Quarr Hill Farm, famous for being the place where the Frome Hoard was discovered in 2010, to his son William.

When did your grandfather *(pictured left)* come here?

I think he came to Witham as a tenant farmer for the Duke of Somerset just before the war. He moved from Tynemead up to here [Quarr Hill] I think during the war. He had three sons: Reg, my father. Danny's father – Len. And then their brother was Geoffrey Sheppard. I was named after him. He died of meningitis. In this house. During the war, I presume.

Early days at Quarr Hill. Reg Sheppard at the left with his brother Len behind him. Their brother Geoffrey is leaning against the door frame, with Herbie Trollope to the right

Your father and his brothers have just been milking in that picture?

Those canisters are early milking machinery. The chap on the right, Herbie Trollope, had just milked one by hand; he's got the stool and the milking pail. He worked here for some years.

When I was a kid there was a dairy herd on every farm in this village. Even Bill Powell *(the coal merchant at Upper Holt)* had cows up there, Sweetnap had cows, Phil Stevens, the rest of the Stevens. It's virtually all gone now.

You always worked on the farm?

Geoff: Yeah.

Ann: You went away to school as well.

Geoff: To boarding school. Only Warminster. When I come to the end of my secondary education, because I'd been boarding since the age of eleven, all I wanted to do was come back and work. I didn't want to do any more education, 'cause I wanted to come home! The idea with my father was that if he sent me to boarding school then I might see things differently; not necessarily want to come home farmin' – but o'course it had the opposite effect because I was away from it and so I wanted to come home more'n ever.

Ann: But then he wanted you to go because you'd failed your eleven-plus, didn't you? Because you had pneumonia.

Geoff: Well, yeah. That was hardly the reason…

Ann: I remember your mum saying he was so cross about it all, and the school felt you were a very capable lad and you should 'a passed it but you'd been ill and they wouldn't take it into consideration. So he decided he would send you to Warminster School rather than go into Frome to school.

Geoff: Well, basically he paid for a grammar school education is what it amounted to. Because in those days you know there was quite a stigma, a sort of dividing line between secondary [modern] education and grammar school education. Which we all look upon it now and say that was totally wrong. There shouldn't be two classes of society and people. Back in those days everybody aspired to go to grammar school, didn't they? If they possibly could.

Ann: I can remember my mum saying to me I wan't allowed to go down and play with some of the village kids – "You've got your own family at home on the farm." So it was a bit like that.

Geoff: I'll always remember father, he said he wanted to play for the Chilcompton football team but his father said, "No no, you don't want to go down playing with all them rough old miners." He didn't want his son playing with them. Lot o'rough old miners playing football! My father had the totally opposite view when I left school. He always made sure I could play football on a Saturday af'noon simply because his father had never let him when he was that age.

Ann: You're saying as well, because your gran'father was a Methodist lay preacher they weren't allowed to do any 'unnecessary work' on a Sunday, were they? They weren't allowed to haul the hay in or anything like that.

Geoff at Witham school in 1959, aged seven

Geoff: Well, not when they were young. Not when their father was still boss. In later years they just said "Silly old fool" and carried on. But certainly when they were youngsters they wouldn't be allowed to do any work on the Sunday. If the hay was fit on a Sunday and it was going to rain on the Monday, then it stayed there and it rained on the Monday, like. Because that's how it was. And the same with drinking. And swearing. My father or my Uncle Len. I mean, I never heard either of them swear…

Ann: They made their own versions. Flicking…or ruddy!

Geoff: Their father would'a just gone wild if he'd heard anybody swear. That was against the Methodist doctrines. I know father said they used to go to dances and they were afraid to have a drink or anything in case that got back to their old man – I don't know to what age that would'a carried on; I s'pose eventually they got old enough to say "Blow the old man, we'll do what we want to do" but certainly in their teens or early twenties p'raps…that was what they thought.

Was the farm predominantly dairy when you started work here?

Geoff: Danny's father farmed New House Farm: my father farmed this; there's always been a dairy herd here – Uncle Len, he had a dairy herd up there as well and they both used to grow a bit of corn cos we've got some dry ground here that will grow corn. My father and uncle continued in the partnership after my grandfather died. They bought New House Farm and bought Quarr Hill Farm [but] as soon as they'd paid off for both farms they split up the partnership and went their own ways. I suppose they must've got on reasonably well; as brothers sometimes do they can't always see eye to eye so they split up and went their own separate ways.

Geoff's father in the yard at Quarr Hill Farm. *"That would've been 1958 or 7 I reckon. Cos thas taken in our old yard, all unrecognisable now cos it's concreted over with different buildings but that there was the old pigsties. As you can see they were fallin' down before they pushed it down and put a decent building up. The yards weren't concreted then; just hardcore you know; the cows were housed in the winter in these old cowstalls then, tied up by their necks and milked."*

Witham's got some dry ground?

Geoff: All this up through here is all stone brash, this ridge, all up the way through to Wanstrow. During the war, they had the thrashing machine for the War Ag. Must've been fairly early on, cos I think their brother Geoffrey was alive then, and they would run that as a contracting business. Geoffrey was in charge of it. They had to go around all the local farms doing the thrashing, basically, cos each area was allotted a thrashing machine. Used to have a big old American International tractor with a great big winch on the back because they'd tow this thrashing machine around in the winter, to thrash these ricks out, and of course on wet ground they'd have to pull him out with the winch and tractor, to get him out of the field, I suppose!

Ann: So you could remember the thrashing machine still being there when you were a boy?

Geoff: I can remember the last rick they thrashed here. I was only about five then. I remember coming home one night from school and the thrashing machine was no more. The scrap merchant had come and he'd beat the thing up, left the wood behind and took all the metal away. I can remember them cutting the last piece of corn with the old binder as well – they would've had to, to have used the threshing machine. We had the old binder here for quite a few years, and then he went, somewhere along the line. It seems such a shame that they beat the old thrashing machine up, because if they'd hung onto him he'd been worth a lot of money.

Did you gradually take over [on the farm] as your father got older?

Geoff: When I left school me father was still boss but he always gave me a pretty free hand to do what I liked, as regards getting the place up together and tidying it up. It was in a bit of a state when I left school. He hadn't had no labour much for several years. In fact, soon after I left

school he'd feed the calves and do the milking and that's what he did for the rest of his farming career. He was never interested in driving the machinery or any of the practical tasks, really.

Ann: But Reg was also untidy, as well, wasn't he…

Geoff: He was a very untidy man, so…*(laughter)*…consequently I am perhaps the other way, because I hate untidiness and a mess. He was a good farmer and a good stockman, a good businessman, but when it came to practicality, he was, ooh – quite a mess here, wan'it?

Ann: Yeah.

Geoff: It was a very gradual sort of a thing, really – by the time he died I was in effect running it but he still held the purse strings and did the paperwork – but I've always hated paperwork anyway!

But to be fair, he always milked. He liked milking his cows and that's what he was good at. The two of us always milked together – the old parlour we had at the time was a two man job. And he couldn't sorta give the milking up so we both milked togther, right until the day he died. That was in February '86, a real awful cold day then; he never had a specific day off, you know, just milked, and if he wanted to go anywhere then he didn't milk. That didn't happen that often, so he was still milking twice a day when he was sixty-seven, an' then that one morning, that was one of those real cold bitter cold winters – he said to me he said, "I don't know, I think I've had enough of this milking now." That was the first time I'd ever heard him say it. And by lunchtime he was dead.

He'd been treated for blood pressure, he said he hadn't been feeling so well, had to go and see the doctor that lunchtime. And thas the only time I ever heard him say that he'd thought he'd had enough of the milking, and like I say, by the lunchtime he'd had a heart attack, and that was the end of it.

On your journeys have you heard much about the Witham Home Guard?

Quite a few of the interviewee's fathers were in the Home Guard.

Geoff: My dad was and Uncle Len was. Nearly all the farmers were in the Home Guard. There again, I wish I'd a few more stories out of them about that. I know they had a prisoner of war working here during the war. They had a German here.

Ann: Where did he live then?

Geoff: I don't know where he lived. Now there again, see, I heard these odd bits but never thought at the time to delve into more detail. Trouble was you see Father died when I was thirty-four and in those days I didn't have the interest, the same interest in local history [as I do now]. Of course, thirty years is a long time since – I'm absolutely history mad now! A lot of this came from me Uncle Len rather than me father cos Uncle Len, he liked to have a bit of a jaw, chat, like…I remember him saying the prisoner of war they had here at the end of the war, they said they felt ever so sad for him when he had to go home because he had to go back to East Germany. He was worried to death to go back and wondering what he would find, his family and all. He would've rather stayed here than go back.

Ann: We've still got that toasting fork here that he made, haven't we? S'posed to've been made by a prisoner of war. It's in the pantry.

Geoff: John Nicholls over there *(nods in the direction of Barrow Hill Farm)* when I used to go over there as a kid, his father had a wooden 'plane: a model on top of their cabinet in the kitchen. Apparently that was made by a German prisoner of war that used to work there. The other thing I remember father telling me was that a Hurricane had crash-landed up in Postlebury during the war. He said "We went up and had a look.

Well, the pilot were there on the floor, obviously dead. I'd never seen a dead person before. He had a moustache. There were nothin' the matter with him, he looked perfect, wasn't shot about or anything like that." I never thought no more about it, I thought p'raps that was one of his stories, you know. But not so many years ago I bought a book *'Somerset at War'* – in the back all the aircraft that ever crashed in Somerset are listed. There's about half a page of German ones - and there's hundreds of Allied aircraft, page after page after page! So I looked through that and sure enough there's a Hurricane crashed Cloford or Postlebury and they give the pilot's name and the unit 'ee come from, Yeovilton, I think. [Father thought at the time] it was the result of a crash due to a air pocket rather than enemy action. That was a little story he told.

Ann: Uncle Len used to laugh and say about the Home Guard. Uncle Len had osteomyelitis, didn't he, years ago in his hips, he had one leg quite a lot shorter than the other and he used to wear a caliper and things.

Geoff: One of the Coxes was the sargeant, trying to do his job properly, like. They had to stand up on parade and Uncle Len, he weren't standing to attention very well, cos he had this bad leg so called. You know what it's like, young blokes get together, old sargeant says, "Oh well, can't you stand to attention any better than that? Can't you?" And he says, "Well no, I can't, I got this bad leg." Sargeant said "It ain't good enough" and Uncle Len said, "Well, tis good enough for me!" Course, he had a bit of a strop on about it, the sargeant, and said, "Well, what's the point of me being the sargeant if you ain't going to take no notice of what I'm tellin' 'ee?" And one of the other wags down there said "Well thas all right then, you needn't be the sargeant any more, we'll have they stripes off you," so they cut his stripes off!

Another time they nearly caught the station on fire…

Ann: Probably having a brew up, I expect! I remember my dad saying he was on fire watch, and he used to have to go on at Cranmore Tower and he said alls he ever learnt really was to drink cider – didn't do much else!

Geoff: Leonard always used to like telling a story about the wood – about the dead German pilot hanging in his parachute harness up in the trees up in the wood on the top there – until one of the forestry workers found him. Course, Leonard used to like to say there was a gamekeeper or a forestry worker that had a spaniel and the spaniel come back to his owner one day with a bit of German, like, cos he'd been hanging there in the trees for so long, but that might have been his invention…I know he was found in the wood cos it's in one of the local history books… but Leonard liked to elaborate these things.

I do wonder if there's any of that Hurricane left up there, though…

Geoff: Well, funny you should say that. All that ground was left to rack and ruin, wan't it? For ever. And then last year or the year before, Timmy Crees was busy renting it out so nearly all of it now have bin ploughed up. Anyway, young Snookie in the village – you know, the contractor kiddie – he comes here quite often…I didn't put it to him at all, he just said to us, he said "I've bin ploughin' up some of that up there, you won't believe it. In one of those hedges, there's a plough halfway up a tree." That plough was abandoned there in the hedge. Stuff'd just get left there for ever. And that tree must've took the plough up with it. As it grew up, the plough was up in the air. At the same time he said there was a plane that crashed up there as well and he'd ploughed up some ammunition cases. I spoke to him about it and said, "Is that all?" He said "We think we might've ploughed a bit of propeller up." I hadn't put it in his head, and I said, "Well I know what you're talking about cos I've heard this said before that this Hurricane crashed up there." So he actually ploughed the site and ploughed up one or two bits and pieces. So I said "Where are they now?" He said, "Well, on Timmer Crees's workbench."

Shotguns and pitchforks form an archway as newly-weds Geoff and Ann Sheppard walk out of Christ Church, Frome in 1977

Ann: Should find out where it was, go up for a walk up round.

Geoff: You've sure'n heard of the bad winter when all the farmers took the milk down to the station to get it away in the '62/63 winter? I can remember taking the milk down, puttin' the churns on the train, all the farmers gettin' down the station with their milk, and having great big snowball fights! I was only about nine or ten – funny how things stick in your mind when you're young. I remember being hit by a snowball… in the side of the face, and that bloody hurt! Almost crying with this snowball. This farmer had hit this little nine year old. Thas always stuck in my mind ever since, for some reason…

I remember seeing a bit of ciné film of that winter, [cousin] Tom's ciné film. They had some [footage] of it there, the snow up New House, a little grey Fergie trying to get out with some hay and a cart to feed the cattle out in the field. Spinning like hell in the snow, like. I must see if he's got that [transfer from ciné] sorted out. Because that'd be ruddy wonderful. To see your parents as they were, young people. I remember seeing my mother on it. She was snow white as far back as I can sort of remember now, but on this cine film she had this sort of real dark black hair like, you know.

There was cheese making down Tynemead. You knew they made cheese down at Tynemead at one stage? Brian Bullock's sister Beryl used to work down there. I remember when we were at Witham school going there on a visit to see the cheese making when Mr Jakins was there. He always used to make cheese. First time I'd ever seen cheese being made. We used to have nature walks as well. These little details that come to mind. Playing rounders in the field at the back of the school in the summer, like. Basically where Hutton's houses are now. Just out there. An' if you went on out across that field, afore you got to the hedge, there used to be quite a big gully there that we used to play in when we were at school, like lunchbreak.

Mr Gartell used to farm Manor Farm when I was a kid. Then the Griffins came first and then the Jowetts. The Jowetts, they milked cows there. Right up to the early eighties, I suppose? There must've been a dairy there until milk quotas came in, which was 1983 and then Jowetts left the village soon after that. Most of the cottages in the village belonged to either the Jowetts or Yeomans as regards thas where the workers lived. As I say, when milk quotas came in, that sort of heralded the start of the change really.

When Jowetts sold up, Alan Dibben bought the whole lot. He was the one that sold it all off, split it all up if you see what I mean. If I remember rightly he bought the lot as one, and then sold the cottages off and sold the farms off all separately and of course thas when the village changed really. Up until then, all their workers were living in the village, participating in village events, and then when those two big units were sold off we had the start of the change really – I don't like using it, but – when the newcomers started coming in, if you know what I mean. Well, people wanted to live out in the country, didn't they?

When I was young there was a period when a lot of the farmworkers, they were wantin' to get into Frome, get jobs in Frome, their wives wanted to be where the shops were, instead of cocked out in the countryside and of course in them days they didn't have their own transport. They were reliant on a very sporadic bus service so there was a period in time when a lot of the workers that were working out in the villages wanted to get into the town so that they had all the conveniences on their doorstep, you know. When you think about about it, all these cottages are in such demand and are worth so much money now – like I say, going back to the fifties, before everybody had their own car I mean they were just farmworker's cottages really. Things change, don't they? When we used to go to school we always used to walk down and if the milkman used to come by with the crates o'milk he'd often stop and give us a lift.

Used to think nothing about it. A much simpler age, I suppose. Whereas now, you only got to ask any of these school leavers that come to work for you, walk across the bloody yard – and they look at you as though, you know – they don't want to walk anywhere! If they can't drive, or get on a quad, or… Walking? If you ask them to go and get the cows and walk, it's just unheard of!

Do you think you'll carry on, in terms of work?

What, me meself? As far as I'm concerned I will never retire. I say to people, I'll just fade away, that's how I look at it. I obviously don't want to do as much; I won't be as physically capable of doing it. As long as I'm still useful and welcome out there I'll just go out and do what I want to do.

Do you look back upon that free rein your father gave you and try to do the same for Will?

Yes, I do. Recently I've had this conversation with different people, same sort of age as meself and I say to them "My son's thirty-two and basically he runs the farm now; the last two or three years he's come into his own, he runs it." We discuss it all still, he puts in the ideas of what he wants to do to me; but in effect he does what he wants to do rather than what I want to do – because at the end of the day I've had enough of being the boss, if you like, and if he's going to continue runnin' it then we've got to do what he wants to do because iss 'im is actually going to do it. I say to 'im, as long as he can keep me into me old age, as long as I can still be a bit useful, as long as he can make it pay then he can do as he pleases, within reason.

A few years ago when the dairy farming did go through a really bad patch, I said to William "Well, you're the age now if you really want to do it then we'll stick with it and see how things go – hopefully they're

bound to improve from where they are now – but the most important thing is do you enjoy it?" Cos if you ain't enjoying it then you'll never make a success out of it. If you're a hands-on family farm you do it cos it's a way of life, really, as well as your income. I think a lot of the processors and milk buyers, they know that they'll always have milk because they know that however tough things get, farmers by and large want to stay farming really. *(laughs)* They don't want to give up. I'm not saying the great big industrial size units are; it's more of a business where people make a big investment and want a return on their money same as any other businessman.

Different when you get to my age; I say to people until I was about at least fifty-five or even older, fifty-eight – I'm sixty-two now – no way would you have ever thought you'd want to get rid of your cows or pack it in. But now, if William didn't want to farm I'd sell the cows tomorrow. I could quite easily do that. But ask me to have done that five or six years ago, I just couldn't've contemplated life without it. I would hate to have to sell it now but certainly in the past it would've almost been suicidal if I'd had to have sold it but now if I had to I could accept it. I'd have to sell it and move away from it, but I certainly wouldn't want to… Hopefully we'll see out the rest of my days here cos there's nowhere else I particularly want to live at the moment. Once you get older, whether you change again and think differently, you can't tell. P'raps in a few years time I'll be in a bungalow in Frome where I can walk to the shops, I don't know! *(laughter)*

That is the one thing that saddens me. I'm a bit nostalgic I suppose and interested in history and tradition and all the rest of it, but in this country we 'ad all these nice little farms, especially dairy farms, little units that were all capable of producing an income for a family. Now a lot of them have gone altogether and it's all been split up and you see horse paddocks here and horse paddocks there; that nice little uniform system we had.

It was a farming ladder, you know, people could start down the bottom with a few acres with a small unit and if they worked hard they could gradually build up and become big if they wanted to. But that ladder's gone now and like I say a lot of the nice little units – well they're no more now, are they? Because the farms have been wiped off the face of the earth and they've been amalgamated with other units; or it's gone to the leisure industry as regards people buy up for horses. And it just seems sad to me. But then thas just nostalgic I suppose and not necessarily progress, but…

What is the saying? They say if you are a farmer you should farm as though you are going to live for ever and live as though you were going to die tomorrow. Life's a sorta cycle, i'n't it? You know, you see it happening to other friends of mine that are a bit older, you see them going through the same processes only a few years in advance of yourself, like. And when you get there you think, oh, that's what they were going through a few years ago! It's quite funny really looking at life like that. I remember going to dances and things, you know, a few years ago, got friends that were bit older than me and they'd sort of be creeping off about twelve o'clock to start off with and you'd think, "Well, it's going to go on for another hour, what they going on for?" And then a few years later, they're all sort of creeping on at about eleven o'clock, and you think, "What in the world's the matter with them, woss going on?" And now I get anywhere meself an' I think, oh, at about eleven o'clock, have to think about going on in a minute, like. It all happens to everybody.

You're not milking in the morning?

No. Well, we've had this new parlour. I've always milked ever since I left school cos I'd always rather milk than do tractor driving, so I have always milked. Until the last three or four years. Milking had become quite a chore, really, because we had too many cows for the size of the parlour so it required two of us to be in there all the time, just to get it done in a reasonable time, like. Now we've got this new parlour it means that one can manage quite easily on his own so one of us now can do it in half the time two of us used to do before, like. So I don't actually milk as such anymore, I go out when I'm asked to. I relief milk now really and I don't have to get up as early anymore, I don't have to be there to start milking. The winding down process has begun. When all the cattle are in [for the winter] I'll have to get up a bit earlier but at the moment they don't need me to get up if everybody else is here. I keep saying, I travel about and you don't see no livestock out in the field, you don't see no cows out in the field, and somebody said, well a lot of 'em they're housed all year round now. That's why you don't see so much out in the fields. Even beef cattle, I s'pose, housed most of the time now rather than fattened on grass. Everybody's trying to do what they think is most economic for their particular farm and business. Every farm is so different from the next that no one system is necessarily right across the board.

Thank you, Geoff – I'd better think about turning in now – never mind about getting to eleven o'clock!

Well, iss only ten o'clock.

Opposite: Geoff Sheppard and his son William. Quarr Hill Farm, April 12th, 2015

Don Stevens with his elder brother Cliff, circa 1938: *"Thas when Cliff was mending a puncture on an ole Allis B."*

Don Stevens, Farmer, 83

After fifty-four years
it doesn't have much blunt to it…

Now living at Tytherington near Frome, Don Stevens was born at Witham in 1931. His father bought land closer to the village after the second estate auction and built a house, known as Homemead Farm, where Don and and his wife Doris lived until 1981. Their son Philip farmed there until 2006.

Right Don, where were you born and when?

I was born at Moorpark Farm, Witham Friary in 1931. Before that, Father and they came up from down on the Somerset levels in 1929. Father brought the cattle up on the train when they moved to Witham. They brought the heifers up one week and then the next week they brought the cows, I think they milked them in the morning and then drove them to Cheddar station and put them on the train and came up to Witham Friary and then up Moorpark. A two or three hundred acres farm and also some of the rough land up on the top. That used to belong to Witham Park. Nobody didn't farm it so father took it over.

Why did he move from Wedmore?

You know, my father started up on his own cos his father died young – he got kicked or summat an' he had a lot of ulcers come out on his leg. And granny used to say how he always said, if he were gonna die, he were gonna die wi' his leg on. They wanted to have his leg off an' he wouldn't have it. I never knew'n. That left my father and Uncle Tom and Uncle George and Aunt Mabel. They more or less had to fend for themselves. My father, he gradually took they bits of land down on the moor when they did come available.

Well, it was so much wet and that down there, and not only that, you see, you wouldn't have a farm with all the land. I mean, when he left down there he had land in six parishes…two or three fields here and then perhaps three or four over Crickham or somewhere like that, you know. They spent all their time scattered about the place, like, mother and one of them would go milking in one place and father and perhaps my oldest brother would go the other place milking, you know.

So, they're milking out in the fields.

Oh yes! When the floods were in, sometimes, in the summertime, they did drive the pony and cart so far and tie'n up at the gate, get in the boat, row it across the moor, milk the cows and row'n back again! They'd maybe take the milk straight into the milk factory. Some of 'em was ten gallon churns. They had a great big heavy iron band around the bottom, I mean [as if] that wasn't enough, let alone the rest of it too…

Do you still have family on the moors?

Roger Wilkins, his mother's my cousin, he's still there. He'll never alter, you know, he's so Somerset. Like Mike Jagger's brother d'live along the road from him, like, the popstar, an' he d'go on in wi' Roger makin' cider.

Chris Jagger…

He's got his own band and everything. They d'have right old knees-ups sometimes!

He did a gig at Glastonbury recently.

Doris: Do you go to Glastonbury? The festival, I mean.

On the bus from Frome one year, just for the Sunday.

Don: I've been down there – one time, me son, had to go to the Eavises and pick up calfs, you know. And it's an eye-opener to see the work that ever goes in to that, mind, the build-up to a pop festival, lorries, the big lorries with loads and loads of stuff.

One hundred and seventy thousand people?

Don: You wouldn't think they could ever manage to organise it.

Doris: What do you if you're in a crowd like that and if you wanna pee, you just do it, I suppose, do you? I mean the blimmin' facilities… *(laughs)* the mind boggles to what do go on. *(more laughter)* Sorry.

Don: What were it this time? They sold out the tickets in so many minutes?

Doris: Beginning of this week, wan' it?

Monday [6th October, 2014]. Twenty-six minutes.

Doris: Ask me questions, thas the best way. Is that thing on? All this gabble…

What's your earliest memory of Witham?

Don: When I was supposed to go to school and didn't (*laughs*). Cos, now I seem really naughty, but I mean…Miss Hunt had sent me out in the cloakroom for being naughty and I thought "I've had enough and I'm going home so…" (*Everyone laughs*) I were always noted for being a terror because, I mean, if I didn't feel as though I wanted to go to school, I got out the bedroom window and went along the roof and down over another roof, I could hide in there and Mother couldn't see me…

She thought you'd gone to school?

Don: No, she knew I were out there but she couldn't get me out…but that were another thing during the war, when they were desperate for farm work and that, we could have so many half-days [off] from school to help on the farm…

That was a part of the war effort, was it?

Don: Yeah, and the two evacuees that used to lodge down with Mrs Flo Warren [at Rough Stubbs], Fred Deacon and Ron Deacon, they did come as well, having half-days as well to help on the farm when we were hay making and harvesting.

How old were the evacuees?

Don: They were about twelve, went back to Witney just after the end of the war, about '45 or '46, I suppose… We never kept in touch for years. Then one day Ron came in with his car and said "You remember me?"
   I said "No" and he said "You think back 'bout forty-six or forty-seven years," and I thought, well I can't remember that long ago, and he said "Well we were evacuated there," and we've kept in touch ever since.

You probably have a picture of you together when you were young?

Doris: Have we?

Don: You'd better go an' have a look.

Doris: Got wedding photographs…

Don: What happened to them?

Doris: What, in that little book? Thas just when you were knee-high to a grasshopper, in'it?

That'd be perfect.

Doris: He says, what happened to it? Yes, what happened to it?

Don: Well, you do the tidying up…

Doris: The more room you got, the more you d'spread it around…

Seems very tidy to me…

Doris: Ahh, you don't see in the cupboards!

(*Doris leaves and minutes later enters with the photo album*)

Don: Oh dear. Now tis coming out!

Doris: We found this without any bother, but ….we'st forgotten what was in here, Chris…

Don: Well these is some little snapses that me sister took…

Don: Thas when I was goin mowin'! Yeah, you'd take me out an' put me in the field! I weren't very old…

Doris: The old tractor they used to drive, he had to stand up to get the bloody guts [clutch] to go down, course he'd not enough weight…

Don: I spect as usual I had me boots on the wrong feet!

(Doris laughs)

You've still got the same cheeky smile.

(More laughter)

Doris: It's the teeth gone now!

(Even more laughter)

That's a rick and that's you with your hand on the cider [flagon]…

Don: Yeah. An' there's the old elevator…an' thas a old fashioned hay collector, you see – what used to pull the hay in, with the horse.

Doris: Don had a head o'white hair, you know, really blondy blondy. Well, tis only in the photographs – I didn't know'n then.

Don: See, mother had one or two white cockerels, and they din't like me, they did chase me an' get on me back…

Doris: Cos you'd bloody torment 'em! They reckoned they used to make you what d'you call sugar dummies; used to put sugar in a bit o'rag for to suck an' 'ee reckoned 'ee was goin' round with this in his mouth an' he did drop it an' the blimmin old cock would run away wi' it! An' he was stood there bawling cos the sugar dummy were gone!! Thas goin' back a bit!!

I'm sure we don't realise the stupid daft things that used to go on din'it, an' you know an' how primitive it was, really. *(points to album and Don).* You'ven't seen'm for a long time, I reckon!

Overleaf, photo right:
Don: *"Thas how they did get to cut out the hay from the ricks. With the hay knife."*
Doris: *"Almost wedged shape sort of blade, weren't they?"*
Don: *"Thas Treacle or Blossom, I reckon. Cos father used to have six horses, like two what he brought up from down on the moor, used to drive milking an' that, you know, cobs, an' four big cart horses for to do the big heavy work, you know."*

Overleaf, photo left: After the ceremony, seen here in the garden of the Seymour Arms. Don aged seven, holding the train of his brother Cliff's new wife, Mary, on Monday April 18th, 1938. Back row: Charles Stevens, Leslie Stevens, Joan Stevens, Mr Gingell (Mary's father). Front row: Mrs Stevens, Violet Stevens, Clifford Stevens, Mary Stevens née Gingell, Don, Mrs Gingell & Gran Tompkins

[Did] Miss Hunt [at Witham] ever give you the cane?

Don: The ruler. I was talking [in class] and course, the teacher marched me out the front and I had to hold out both hands.

You would be arrested if you did that now.

Don: Absolutely. Anyhow, as I went back, the other kids and I were talking, as I went back, I went like that *(makes face)* and the teacher said – "What's the matter with you?" – said he – "Hit me miss!" – I had two, and she said – "now go back and sit in the corner" – and I said no and I had two more *(laughs)*. But you respected the teacher, and now the teachers are treated horribly, aren't they?

She [Miss Hunt, the Witham teacher] lived in Frome did she?

Don: She used to come out everyday on the train, that's as far as I can remember, and then she married Mr Cunnington.

That must have been quite a surprise.

Don: Yeah, because she was quite elderly, and there used to be another teacher who used to teach the young ones, Kath Phillips, that used to teach the little ones. Then during war time, they had another; Miss Williams, took on from Kath.

So Mrs Cunnington was quite a strict teacher then?

Don: Yeah, she was a good teacher.

But no nonsense.

Don: No, lessons were lessons, you know. Which they should be – that's where all the trouble is now, because they've got no discipline at home, the parents are out working and they just do what they want to. I mean, I had got home from school and I would go and do jobs; get the second lot of cows [for milking] or something.

And you would have already walked down from Moorpark in the morning and would have walked back again in the afternoon.

Don: Yeah, three miles.

Did you take a packed lunch?

Don: Yeah. And when I would get home I had to get the cows in…

Do you remember the winter of 1947 at all?

Don: I think that that was the year it rained and froze, and you could hear all the branches coming off the trees with the weight of the ice on them. Yeah, that was, 'cos I know Ren, me brother and I went off to do the milking and he did go off to the cattle and feed them and made sure they had something to eat, and he reckons they did crackle because of the ice on them.

Doris: On their jackets, hmm.

How did you meet?

Don: Well that was…

Doris: Just a minute, what I'm going to say is, was that before the tug of war down at Witham, or after?

Don: That were before, when I used to come up an' get the….that was Witham fete! That was later on.

Doris: I couldn't remember which way round it was. *(laughs)*

Don: Like, my father, he was always buying stuff for cattle, he'd always look at it as the cattle had to have what they wanted an' he bought a big clamp o'mangles…

Doris: Manglewurzels!

Don: ….up at Maiden Bradley, an o'course I had to go up there wi' a tractor an' trailer an' get a load. Then somebody came there.

Doris: They were stacked down the bottom, over the hedge from me and my dad's land. Laurel Farm, woss fell down now. Just below the crossroads on the Frome road. There was a little old farm down in there. We had the milk round in Maiden Bradley for nearly twenty year, dad and I. We come from Dorchester, mum as well, like. He always wanted a smallholding to work on, he used to look after an old gent, he had some cows and a big garden an' like that. Then we come up, rented this from the Duke – dad nearly turned round an' went back because it was just nothing but brambles. 1941 or '2, summat like that. He started up the milk round. I was only five or six then.

He started by taking pails of milk round and they'd come to the door with the jug an' measure the milk in. Then we went to bottles – dad used to pull a four wheel trailer around – dad never drove, he didn't know the first thing about it. We bottled it by hand. We were there til 1957 – when I got married.

So this young man with a tractor and trailer…

Doris: These mangles were the other side of the hedge, the hill did come back down a bit from the Frome road. Father'd sent me to Stourhead, they had a, teaching you how to put this strychnine down these holes, to catch these moles, so called, an' I were on me bike over to Stourhead (don't look at me like that) there was just a little course to show you what to do, you know, how to…

Don: Get the worms in.

Doris: …you'd get the worms and put them in this…

Don: Put the powder on 'em.

Doris: Put these worms down the holes for to kill the moles. An' thas what I was down there doing, down at the bottom of the hill. Cos he was the other side of the hedge and I sort of went over an' had a little chat, you know.

Don: Then we didn't have much doing, not til Witham fete.

Doris: Yeah. At the Witham fete.

Don: I suppose tug of war for Witham.

Doris: Thas right, yeah. I shall always remember Don walking up under arch an' o'course he'd been playing tug of war, well he had on great big hobnail boots an' I can sort of hear them now, CLONK, CLONK, CLONK, off in under the railway!

Had you walked down from Bradley?

Doris: No. Dunno how I got there. Must've been pushbike, I spose. Then he used to pushbike up to Bradley to see me, like after that, you know…

Don: I used to ride a bicycle from Witham to Maiden Bradley, up over Private Road *(from Upper Holt Farm to Yarnfield Gate)*, and then come back some nights…come back, I mean at perhaps half past ten, eleven o'clock at night – pitch black.

Doris: …about five or six year afore we got married.

Don: Cos they wanted us to stay at home, see, cos of the work.

Doris: What, mother an' father? Oh yeah, yeah, yeah. When we were courting it was a job to find him because he was always working. *(laughs)*

Don: I wish I could've done more work! *(laughs)*

Doris: After fifty four years it doesn't have much blunt to it! *(laughs)*

Don: You were on about getting married. And then her uncle an' auntie used to live here and they decided to retire, her father bought it and they moved down here from Maiden Bradley after we got married.

Doris: I lived here for a fortnight from the fourteenth of October. I went to Bradley an' got married and then come back an' lived at Witham. I come back here after my mum and dad died in 1981. Would you like a coffee? *(Sound of kettle boiling, three mugs being stirred)*

Doris: Would you like some rum in it?

(Interviewer glances at clock, decides it's too early) No, thank you!

Doris: Like I said before you come, we haven't got any photographs because in that time….work. That was the main… yes, we got photographs of the kids and things like that but I mean you never thought about taking a picture of what was goin' on on the farm or anything…it was all work. Well, my dad and his dad, all they ever *(raps table)* was…I mean people say about hobbies but no, work, you know.

Don: My father…they had a saying down Witham: Moorpark is where they work until they'm tired, and then they get up and start again! Down the village, they had a saying!

Doris: So we've met – where we going now?

Homemead was built for you because your brothers had the other two places?

Don: The ninety odd acres what we made into a farm used to belong to Manor [Farm], down by the church. An' George Gartell, that went into the syndicate with father an' they when they bought. When the Duke had to sell it. An' then whether he couldn't afford it or what, he turned round and sold the ninety odd acres to help pay for down by the church. Thas when father bought it. Well, then took us two or three year to get planning permission to build a house there.

Doris: We had that, you know. We were given that. Dad put up the house, the house cost two thousand quid (they knocked it down not long ago).

Don: Then he said "I built the house for you, now you got to do the best you can." So then we had to turn round and when we could afford it, we did put up another building, you know, that was how we built the farm.

Don and Doris get married at Maiden Bradley Church, October 1957.
Don's father, Charles Stevens, is in the back row on the far left

Doris: We started off with a little herd of Ayrshires, didn't we, you and I? Used to do our own bit and walk across to Moorpark twice a day an' help with the main milking over there.

Your father was still alive then?

Doris: Mum died in '66, dad died in....'70? Vi would know.

Your brother stayed at Moorpark?

Don: Ren did, yeah. He died Frome Show day – we only said the other day, when the year was it? That was a brain tumour.

Doris: Twelve year ago I spec.

Don: Yeah. He worked hard, all his life.

Doris: Cliff died first, then Ren, then Les.

Don: Les, my eldest brother went up to Maiden Bradley.

Doris: And all his family is still up there. But Don and Vi is the only ones that were born at Witham, all the others were born down on the levels.

Don: Well, they'm on now about no young farmers comin' on. But you see, Maiden Bradley estate, when a farm did come vacant, they did put it all on Les's, me brother's – an' thas how – now, they got about six places between them.

Doris: Yeah, cos they got the land where we [me & my parents] were.

Don: A little place like their little place, about forty acres. Ideal for a couple that just want to start [farming], or anything, or interested; and down on the Somerset Levels, the Somerset County Council have sold all the [council] farms down there.

So, what about these tunnels then Don?

Don: Well, um, Denis Wase. He used to work for us.

Doris: Kerry Croft he lived.

Don: And he used to work at Farmer Hoddinott's, out at Witham Hall Farm. He said that he reckoned there used to be a tunnel from out there to the parish room down in the village. I don't know if you've ever been in there and all, down where Denis [Miles] lives now they reckon that's were the monks used to...

Doris: He lives in the old bit in the back. They used to store cattle feed and that in it, until needs be and they done it up.

Don: ...there is one of the biggest coppers you've ever seen, he's about a yard and four foot across. He's huge, isn't he? I mean they used to boil up pig spuds when they did pigs there. But that's what they reckon the old monks used to do their washing in.

1963...

Don: When we had that very bad weather, um, I mean, the wind was quite rough and it [the snow] filled all up our road, up to Homemead and that. I mean that was filled right up, higher than the hedge, and we couldn't get out for the first day or two.

It was easier to go over the fields than it was down the road?

Don: Yeah, because all the snow had blown into the road. I an' Cliff an Gordon and Brian [Stevens, Don's brother and nephews], I mean what we done to get the milk onto the train – where the snow was as high as the hedge, we did make a hole in the hedge an' go out in the field and down across the field then make another hole an' get back out again! Thas how we hauled the milk down onto the train!

You normally had a lorry?

Don: Yeah, it would come and collect the milk, but there was no way to get into Witham, you see, and would start up at Bill Powell's and up Ren's [at Moorpark] then down to pick up ours. [So instead] we'd take it down and put it on the train, and they did unload it at Frome station, cos the milk factory then was right by the station. Express Dairy, where the builder's merchant is now.

And after we'd done the milk hauling, Bill Powell and Paul Phelps, what used to work for us, they'd have our tractor and transport box and deliver coal all around the village when it was wanted. Cos Bill he did only have a lorry, couldn't get out! Poor old Paul and Bill, they did go round, deliver this coal to the poor old women. Flo an' Annie, where Robert [Ludgate] is now. Poor old souls, nobody did know they were there, practically! I mean...they couldn't get out, and there were a shop in Witham then. All the time the bad weather was, I did do their shopping. They would make up a list and I would do it. Course, they were worried that they couldn't get out to get their pension to pay, and I said "Don't you worry about that" and after the snow went, do you know those two old ladies wrote down everything that I got for them. They knew to the exact penny...

How long did it last then?

Doris: I reckon nearly two months. We were hauling the milk the thirty-first of December to January the eighth which is only, you know, nine or ten days. That was when it was bad, when [the lorry] couldn't get there. Five churns, it must have been forty odd gallons a day then. We had to pay eight shillings and a penny to the railway for those five churns to be delivered to the milk factory every day.

The railway invoice for delivering Don's milk to the dairy in Frome from December 31st 1962 to January 8th 1963. The first load contains two days milking as Don didn't get to the station on December 30th because of the snow. The total of four pounds and five shillings is equivalent to £80 today. A year later, freight services from Witham station were withdrawn

Those days of longstanding farming families are gone.

Don: When you say that, Martin, there was a funny story. One night we were in there milking and this lorry pulled up, and a chap come in and he said – "Homemead?" I said yeah, and he said – "oh thank goodness, at last! Every farm I've stopped to so far has said they're Stevens!"

It must have been a bit sad to see Homemead knocked down...

Doris: Yeah, it was very sad. I wish now, when Anne said – "Have you got any photos at home?" and I thought "Flipping heck I haven't," you know, cos Margaret [Stevens] came one time and said, "they took the roof off" – and I thought, you know, do I want a picture of it? I didn't do anything about it, you know, I just felt down and didn't want to know, you know, but now I sort of, perhaps, wish I had.

I suppose you've got photographs of the family outside it, and around the place?

Doris: Well Philip *(her son)*, I said to Philip, "You've got some" and he said that he got pictures – I mean he got the sale brochure and all that which would show the house and everything. I said, "Well it's no good to ask you to bring that now" because he'd forget everything I asked him, you know, because he's so work and work and work, you know. Up the market, everyday. PLA, Premium Livestock Association – that's who runs the market, like...

Is he enjoying it, or does he wish he was back farming?

Doris: Oh no, I think he's enjoying it, I mean, you know, it's hard work, he's self-employed and if he don't work, well, then he don't get paid. But it's so much more company, he knows so many more people in the west of England now than he'd ever have met having stayed where he was, you know. I didn't want Philip to sell, but now with things the way they are I'm glad he did.

Don & Doris Stevens at Toll House Farm, Tytherington. October 10th, 2014

Margaret Trussler visiting friends in Witham. April 12th, 2014

Margaret Trussler, 92

It seemed like a different world down here, everything quiet and peaceful but for the railway station - that was almost modern! You could feel the movement of it all.

My name is Margaret Trussler and I was born in 1922 at Home Farm, Stourton, which was in actual fact on the estate of Sir Henry Hoare in Wiltshire. Just on the other side of the estate was Witham Friary but that was of course owned by the Duke of Somerset and that was in Somerset, but it seemed to us like another part of, well, two friendly estates.

Did anybody from Witham Friary work at Home Farm?

No, because they would be employed by the Duke of Somerset whereas our people were all employed in the village [Stourton]. I think nearly every-one was employed by the land owner. Everything was quite feudal then.

What are your earliest memories?

Of having a happy childhood and being among the animals. We always had help in the house which was from a girl – Elsie Snook, there was another one called Ivy – I suppose a mother's help really who invariably came from Witham Friary. She would come on her bicycle and live in and then when she had an afternoon off invariably would say; "Would you like to come down to Witham and see my house?" and we had the privilege of going into some of the cottages here. There were hardly any cars in those days and there was a white gate across the track by the lodge at the top of *Private (the road from Upper Holt Farm to Yarnfield Gate)*. I never remember being charged for going down there but you had to be very nice to the people at the top.

What were the cottages like inside?

Well, they always had a nice atmosphere and seemed homely and all the people in the actual village seemed friendly; as if they had time to spend with you. They would be standing at their gates and saying: "Oh, who are you and what have you come for?" – "We've come to see so and so," and [then] "have you seen the trains?" and we always said; "well, yes we like to go and watch the trains!"

What did Elsie do at Home Farm?

Oh, she was a general help. She would get us up in the morning and say "Time you were all dressed and ready for school." Then she would go off and cook the breakfast or help my mother and do house cleaning in the day. She wouldn't do outside work – the farm houses were quite big.

Did she live in?

Yes, yes, [she] had a half day on a Wednesday, bicycling back to Witham Friary. Sunday afternoon off one week and a whole day off on a Sunday the next week. A pretty tough life.

Were you children expected to work on the farm?

No. I think we would have liked to have done, but no, we were forbidden. Nowadays, of course, children aren't allowed because of the health and safety and all the machinery but the thing that attracted us was to get among the animals. Even so my father wouldn't allow it until we were about nine or ten. So we had domestic pets but we weren't allowed to go and interfere with the farm.

Did you go to school in Stourton?

We went to a little private school at Kilmington. I was going to say opposite the shop but the shop's no longer there. Looking back, it seems incredible how one teacher taught just my three sisters and about four other children. Never more than that and she saw us right through our education. She was really like a governess. Looking back I admire her so much, how she catered for all the different subjects and we were all so well behaved, I don't think we would have dared've done anything wrong, and yet she wasn't an old so and so, she was just, uh, you wouldn't dream of doing anything wrong.

Alfred's Tower is very near to Home Farm.

Oh, Alfred's Tower… charabancs as they were called then used to come from miles around with the school children for a day out and there were two lodges at the entrance to the drive up to the tower, owned by some lovely old people called May. One side of the gate they lived in a little lodge and on the other side was the sweet shop and lemonade. We called it a bottle of pop. This lovely old lady, she would let us go in there and choose our sweets from the jars and then you could go and climb the tower which was two hundred and eleven steps up to the top. It was meant to have been built as the highest point in Wiltshire, only [for them] to discover that it was then in Somerset, so that's why it was called the Folly. It's always been a landmark for miles and miles around.

Now it's National Trust, owned by the National Trust and it is used for people for walking and carriage parties and different organisations,

A view of Witham from the railway station, photographed before the Great War

but strangely enough [Stourhead House then] was just a rabbit warren and all the rabbits were reared in there to feed the staff of all the people in the house. In the mansion…but those days are gone.

Was all the farm haulage done by horses?

Oh, definitely – up until the mid-thirties. All during the twenties everything was horse drawn: all the wagons; the ploughing; the milk; it was years before we had a lorry or a tractor or anything like that. I remember there was a time when the milk from Home Farm had to come to Witham station. It normally went to Gillingham station which was in Dorset and for some reason that became uneconomical – so they were to bring the milk right down to Witham station which was a journey of about seven miles and that would be done in ten gallon churns with a brass plate on there – it was about a hundred gallons that would all be brought down by horse and cart and put on the train to London and taken to the United Dairies.

Did you sometimes come down with the cart to see it loaded?

My father did have a car, he was one of the few people who did. He would say, "I'll take you down my little girls and just show you where the milk goes." We didn't actually come on the trailers or anything like that…but we would be brought down and taken for a pretty ride, call and see one or two of his friends down here and that would be a little outing for us.

What do you remember of Witham station?

Oh, just sitting and waiting to watch the occasional train. If there happened to be anybody younger with us we used to say, "Here they come, I think it's coming!" and then make the noise as the train would go and it would be, you know, quite the little education, and terribly exciting, just to see a train coming into the station and the guard getting out and waving the flag and everything's aboard and off they'd go, and we thought that was exciting. It was a junction, and so…well it seemed like a different world down here, everything quiet and peaceful but for the railway station and that was, you know, almost modern (*gasps*). You could feel the movement of it all.

Did you ever go by train from Witham?

Yes, yes I did, we'd just go to Frome. Yes, that was a great outing. [Or] you could go to Castle Cary and then father would pick us up. It was quite fun.

You have a good story about your 21st birthday party.

During the war I was away most of the time nursing and when I was back to my sister in Frome my father said to me "Wouldn't you like a party?" and I said of course, I'd love a party – he said "Well, you can have the barn back at Stourton, we'll make it nice, there won't be a lot of food" (because food was very strictly rationed), "have a little get together, bring all your friends!" Well, it was only my girlfriends that we could muster up really because all the chaps were away in the war and so we all cycled over which was about twelve miles and the barn had been beautifully decorated but he said: "You can't all dance with each other so I've got another treat for you. I've invited all the chaps from the Zeals aerodrome, the young officers, so make the most of it and enjoy yourselves!"

And so, we thought this was very, very exciting and we didn't know, really, how to set about introducing ourselves, so somebody had the bright idea of sticking names on our backs and we had to stick to our partner. Well, it depended who you got but I was lucky so they said "You can be Juliet" and they picked me out a lovely Romeo! Then I had the next day off, clearing up after the party. Now when I got back on the wards the

Witham station in the nineteen-twenties, as Margaret would have seen it in her childhood

chaps sort of said to me: "We hear you had a party, you lucky girl." You know, poor chaps, all lying around with their wounds and things, and I said yes, and "we hear you didn't put in an appearance in the next day."

I said "I'm quite aware of that, but I did do my bit." Anyway, that was quite a nice little interlude from...mmm, from some of the things that weren't quite as nice during the war.

Did you marry a local man?

No I didn't. He came from Frome and he was stationed at the White House in Frome. My sister ran a little coffee shop in Bath Street and I used to go and help her. They came [in] and you'd never believe it, they came in for coffee every single morning when they weren't on manoeuvres and after six months he was the one who said "Would you like to go out one evening?" and so from then on...it was just all go. He was so fun and fell in love with the surroundings here and the life that went with it. We got married and he qualified as being a land agent – that's how we came to stay for over fifty-six years.

Wow, that's wonderful.

That was, so you got that one, didn't you! *(laughs)* Where you begin at the head of the valley there, the terrace drive through to Alfred's Tower from Stourton, that's actually where we started our married life. Nobody else would live there then and now it's the most expensive and sought after place you could think of. So we were very, very, lucky.

Yarnfield Gate is another beauty spot around here.

I remember as children it would be a treat to go there and have a picnic, enter by Yarnfield Gate and walk to your right, across through there and see the Witham Vale valley below. It was an absolutely beautiful view. And the wild rhododendrons: the ponticum was planted either side and you were actually allowed to pick some of it and take some home, whereas at Stourhead you weren't allowed to touch a single bloom. We thought that that was an enormous treat, every holiday time in the spring to take friends there, have a picnic, and then walk all the way through.

Are there any other places near Witham that you have particularly fond memories of?

Batcombe would be another beauty spot, there again it would be just to go and see the primroses. They seemed to just grow anywhere there; banks and banks and banks of them, and that would be an early sort of April trip, driving through the lanes to go and see them, such were the joys of driving in those days. Driving through the country lanes.

Would you say Witham Vale has changed since you were a child?

Not a lot, but all the little pathways have been opened up and the rides and things: thank goodness to all the people who look after the bridleways and footpaths. But apart from [that], the roads and muddy lanes still seem much about the same…a pity about the station though.

Have the farms and the houses changed very much?

Oh, mechanisation has made all the difference in the world. The farms are not as beautiful now because everything is so enormous for housing the machinery; whereas once upon a time the architecture, the buildings, it was all taken into consideration, but now it's all quite ugly – more like enormous hangars or sheds instead of beautiful buildings. I suppose it's much more commercial now. Which is a pity.

Do you remember the hunt coming through Home Farm and Witham?

Oh yes, yes, yes. Oh hunting, it was almost a religion, it really was, because, as it was intended in bygone times, really, you know, for people to be in control of the vermin and they all got together and enjoyed doing it. Well, it was low lying country but the farms were all united. I don't think there was anyone against hunting and they were made so welcome and there would be hospitality offered. When you got up onto the other boundaries right up on the downs and on the way to Salisbury I think they thought people were really rather snooty and stand offish there but down here it was hospitality itself and really genuine friendship.

How often would the hunts take place?

Well, if it wasn't too wet - you couldn't judge it too far in advance – but on a regular basis after Christmas, Christmas through on along to when the season closed which would be about the end of March, beginning of April. I suppose there would be two meets a week in the peak of the season down here, on a Wednesday or Saturday. Depending on the work situation. But I think hunting came first.

Would there always be hospitality at the end of the hunt?

Or to start off with; a stirrup cup of something in one of the farmhouses.

And gymkhanas took place in Witham Friary.

Oh yes, after the hunting season would close, the great event would have been, I suppose, I think there was a flower show down here too, but I don't remember coming to it in actual fact. I do remember the gymkhanas that went right on until my children competed here, that would have been right into the sixties, they had a good run. I think they were absolutely beautifully run then by some people called Sheppard who were farmers. They must have gone to a lot of trouble to have organised it all with the hay making and everything, and yet produced really good, nice little prizes and it was a lovely, friendly thing to do. And if they got into the jump off, which would have been quite late in the evening and the children had already hacked from Stourton and Kilmington all the way down here and then would have to hack back up after a hard afternoon.

A long way, but they loved it. It was the highlight of the holidays! Then there was Mrs Crouch, [did] you know Mrs Crouch? Well, she was a great character and she did so much for the children in encouraging them with their ponies and then she had her husband Norman. He was a farmer. We called him Naughty Norman because he would go on riding in point-to-points, and he was almost forbidden because he wouldn't obey any of the rules and he did all the most outrageous things, risked his own life and, of course, that was why he nearly got chucked out. But nothing would stop him. He appeared and we used to say; "Is Naughty Norman around at the point-to-point?" and there he was, doing something quite scatty. My children still say to me "Do you think Naughty Norman is still alive?" I've no idea. Mrs Crouch – she was a gem with the children, she was so gentle and kind. She was always at the back of the hunt, but she would gather in any stray youngsters: "Just follow me, dear, you'll be fine."

Witham gymkhana, seen here in the early nineteen-seventies

So there was a gymkhana – were there other social events in Witham?

There must have been…

The pub's always been a feature of the village.

Oh my goodness me, if only one could repeat the tales, you wouldn't have to go any farther than that, would you?

Norman Crouch, Farmer, 88

Life's how you make it, isn't it?
If you make it hard for yourself
you've got to put up with it.

The view from Strap Lane overbridge towards Grazemoor Farm in early 1964

Norman was born in London in 1925 and first farmed at Camberley, marrying in 1943, later moving to Somerset. He sold his farm at Hinckley Point in 1961 and bought Grazemoor as a farm worker's cottage with land, added buildings and kept a dairy herd. He rode horses since childhood and bred them for most of his adult life. At the age of eighty-eight he still occasionally took to the saddle and drove his car too. He died in December 2014.

I've got a photograph here which is mostly of the railway line at Strap Lane, looking towards Witham and showing the old Brewham signal box...

Yes, yes, that was working for two or three years after I came here. In fact, the daughter that lived at the farm over there *(nods at Little West Barn out the window)* used to go down to the railway station box and they stopped the train for her purposely just to go to Bruton school! Can you imagine that happening today?

Grazemoor Farm circa 1963, with Mr Crouch's handwritten comment on the back of the print shown below:

This is the new building after "brendon bo" had finished thier part the rest is my job.

Was the barn already here?

My building? No, there was nothing there at all. This was the cottage to the farm up the road [Great West Barn] which was three hundred acres, the son didn't want it and the parents decided to sell it off. It was on the market for about two years and I came along and – I didn't want, well, I couldn't afford the three hundred acres; that was the crux of the matter – otherwise I would've bought it. And I bought this hundred acres and this little house here. The rest I put up myself, the buildings and so on; I had that big barn put up and everything underneath it. When I did it, in those days, I mean people were buying a section of that barn, a quarter of

it, adding it onto their existing buildings. The fact that I had no buildings here at all meant that I bought the place that much cheaper, just buying the bare land, 'cause obviously I had to put up buildings so I had that very big barn put up and everything underneath it I put in myself afterwards. It was a good idea; it worked out very well, but you know I was a young energetic mad-brain that went to the bank and borrowed all the money to put up this massive building and people thought "Well, he won't be there very long!" *(much laughter)*

You said you came up from Hinckley Point?

Yes, by Hinckley Point power station. That was what pushed me out, really. I was right on the edge of it. I was on a little country road which was a crossroad, three of them were tarmacked roads and the other one was a track that went up to a farm.

We were very quiet, very secluded, I had the best house in the parish, and when Hinckley Point came along they just cut a new road straight through the fields, didn't bother about the shape the fields were left in afterwards, they just put a new road straight through – you couldn't stop them or anything like that – everybody objected to it but it didn't make a bit of difference, the objections at all; they just went straight where they thought they were going.

And my place was right on the edge of it. Which spoilt it all together, we were there, it was quiet, you'd see a horse and cart go by, you'd had a busy day and next thing, BWHOOSH, WHOOSH! Lorries and God knows what, new roads and big main road right out to Hinckley Point. They thought I was a troublemaker when I started raising opposition to Hinckley Point coming there but nowadays, the old ones [who were] there, they've either moved out 'cause they couldn't stick it or they do look up when I go back there an' seen the odd one who's very old nowadays and they say "You were right, it shouldn't've come here, spoilt the parish!"

So your intention was to find a farm elsewhere in Somerset?

Yes. Dairy, it was all dairy up there [in the new barn I built]. I milked fifty cows up there until the milk quota system came in and the Milk Marketing Board bought back quotas [that] farmers didn't want; it was a hell of a good price they were offering at the time so I decided after I'd been milking for all those years I'd retire from milking and sold the milk quota back to the Milk Marketing Board and invested the money. As far as I was concerned it was a very good bit of luck for me but then not everybody was my age – the younger people, they had to carry on.

What made you choose this place then?

Well, the layout of it, you know, we weren't in a hurry to rush and buy something. We looked around: we went all down as far as Devon, we didn't go to Cornwall, all over Devon, all over Somerset. Wiltshire we looked over: looked at loads of places. Until in the end I decided this was what I wanted. I don't regret it at all. Nowadays I've let most of the land, only on an eleven month basis so that it's not a permanent tenancy; I can always get it back if I wanted to sell the place.

I've been here for fifty-two years. I missed the wife when I lost her. She used to keep the place so spick and span, not like the table is now, loaded with junk.

Many people remember her giving riding lessons.

Mmmm. *(long, long, pause)*

I was eighteen when I got married. People said "Oh, that won't last five minutes, all too young" but it lasted a lot longer than they lasted. Never had any family; the wife wasn't very keen on it. Well, she didn't want any family at all; I couldn't have cared less whether we did or we didn't. Looking back I think, I'd worked so hard to build up something and got no close relation, son or daughter to take it on which is a bit sad really. I'm sure Kirsten will look after it. She'll look after these young horses that I've got out in the fields. Always had horses, right from I was brought up with them as a child. Used to ride them in the point-to-points…did win one race, never went into National Hunt like Wincanton, Newton Abbot, all the big courses. I did ride in one race there that was open to point-to-pointers and I won that one. That's the trophy, there. *(gestures to mantelpiece)* That's a nice one there [too] with the horse going over the jumps. That clock was another one. I don't fancy the clock like I like the others.

Mr Crouch on Cobblers Point at Larkhill Races. May 19th, 1975

That one is from 2009, four years ago. You weren't riding?

Yes, I rode that one! I rode them all. I [still] go to the Hunts now. Kirsten gets the horses all ready for me. I have to go up a concrete block, up in the yard there where I made about four feet square to put on the back of the tractors for extra weight and that's stuck there and I can climb up on that quite easily 'cause there's another stone next to it. I get on that one and she rides the two horses alongside it; leading the one that I'm getting on, so far off the ground I can't get my leg up to the stirrup for one thing, ha, I climb up on this concrete block and fall on top of the horse and we're off! Yes, we go down to the meet at Witham Friary and I go across two or three fields but I can't stick it any longer; the trouble is, you see that I've got so old that I haven't got enough flesh on me to cover my bones and my backside gets absolutely sore on the saddle, so I've got to come home after a couple of fields. I can't sit down [on this chair] here for a couple of days, I've got to sit on the sofa! *(laughs)* But I enjoy it and everybody comes up, talks, and most of the people that hunted when I was really hunting, they'd all given up, they come to the meet in their cars and just walk around or drive around, I'm the only one still on the horse! Captain Mann, have you heard of him? He was the Master of the South & West Wilts for years and years and years. He still goes around in the car but he's very old and very feeble, his wife died a couple of years ago and that hit him pretty bad.

Was Little West Barn Farm inhabited when you first came here?

Oh yes, oh yes. The only way to get to it was down the track here, along the side of my field. But since it's been sold off, the owners over there bought a strip of land alongside a field to get out on the road the other way [to Strap Lane]. So they don't have to worry about opening the railway gates. Which was always a bind. In fact, a couple of years before

I came here two chaps were killed down there – they went over the line with a load of hay and got on the line and the engine stalled on the line and they couldn't get it going quick enough – train come round the bend that they couldn't see, hit it for six and well, it didn't make a bit of difference to the train but there was nothing left of the lorry in the heap of hay, killed the chaps so these people who bought it afterwards, they weren't very keen on using the gates.

Who were the people there then?

Oh, Stevens was the name, old Mrs Stevens. He *(Mr Stevens, Don Stevens' uncle)* was alive when I came here, he died shortly afterwards and she moved out about two years after he died. And then it was sold then, it wasn't re-let, it was sold, because it belonged to an old lady living down Bridgwater way. She'd let it for years before – she lived there originally; when she got too old to farm it herself she let it, lived on the income. I don't know that it was empty for a long time after that; I forget now whether it was or it wasn't. It's got a very big high walled-in garden over there that, quite attractive to the place, in fact the person that owns it now is a professional gardener and that's why she bought the place, to use the big walled-in garden.

You kept breeding horses after you gave up on the dairy herd?

Yes, oh yes. I didn't have a stallion of my own before I came here; we used to send mares away to stud. I bred this one, the mare and foal I put in Frome Show and the foal won first prize out of about half a dozen foals there. I was pretty chuffed about that. I could've had him gelded after a year but I thought it's a bit daft to do that when he's a prizewinner himself, I might as well keep him as a stallion. And so I did and it seemed to catch on, I didn't charge very much for him and I had quite a lot of

A scene at Grazemoor Farm from the late seventies. Meryl Cannon standing at far left with Karen Gale in waterproofs sorting out the saddle on the pony closest to the camera. Helen Stevens comments: *"Looking at the footwear I think this would have been a group of girls holidaying at Sunny Hill [school in Bruton]. They clearly aren't regular riders and their hats are ones that have been borrowed from Mrs Crouch! This would happen several times in the summer holidays - it was all hands on deck to get them sorted out and lead them round the village. Payment was a free ride in the afternoon. The horses were Sugar Foot, Dobbin, Woolly Socks and Bow Tie."*

mares come here after a bit. I think the best year I had was twenty mares here. He's twenty-two years old now, doesn't look it – gallops around like mad, but the he's never done anything so I suppose he isn't worn out...

Your interest was always point-to-point rather than working horses?

Quite. I was quite lucky. I had one or two nasty spills but got over it alright, never went to hospital or anything...I couldn't. One time I put my shoulder out, that's wicked when you put your shoulder out, if you don't go and have it put back properly – and I didn't. I was milking these fifty cows, I just had to go on milking the cows, it was about two years before it got really settled down again. But trying to lift my arm up to put the milking cups on, that sort of thing, well, for a year it was pretty killing. Didn't know whether to pack up or not. *(chuckles)* But it got right on its own in the end.

They've been on about it on the television, these footballers and various athletes are puttin' their shoulders out – they end up going to hospital and having it put back properly. After a couple of months they're back on the field again. I certainly wasn't! Life's how you make it, isn't it? If you make it hard for yourself you've got to put up with it.

Lot of the farmers around here, they didn't want their children to go to the little local school, they wanted them to have a better education and they used to send them off on the train to Shepton Mallet, to the school there. The old lady who lived out in that cottage [Mrs Thane at Pick Barn] would walk across the fields to get to it. The only time they could get their car out there was in the summer when it was reasonably dry. They had to cross two fields and the rest of the time they couldn't get up the hill 'cause it was slippery. She lived out there after her husband died then the parish got worried about her cause she was getting old and frail and they found her an old people's home in Frome. She lived there for about two years before she actually died. Her daughters were wild girls!

Norman Crouch at Grazemoor Farm, Witham. September 19th, 2013

Duncan Gale leaving the Seymour Arms, February 9th, 2014. His son Kevin is leaning against the pub doorway

Duncan Gale,
Agricultural Engineer, 79

We used to get called out at four in the morning – "Oh, me engine, oh, my milking machine don't work"

Duncan was born in Witham in 1935 and married Val in 1963. Apart from a spell in Frome, he has lived in Witham his entire life. His children, Karen and Kevin, live close by; in Witham and Wanstrow respectively.

Duncan, you were born and bred in Witham…

I lived in the houses opposite where the pub is, the ones going the other way, alongside the railway. I was born in 1935. I think I were only a few months old when we went and moved up Rough Stubbs. So they reckon when I was born my father had to walk up to Nunney to get the nurse, you wouldn't dream of it now would you? We had trains here for other stuff but we never had nothing else but bloody pushbikes. Only peoples'd ever have any cars were farmers!

Where did you live at Rough Stubbs?

No. 7 was right on the end but ours was 9; that was two houses into one cos we had a staircase at each end of our house, we 'ad three bedrooms on that one. Then there was 10 and 11; my grandfather an' that was in 11.

Used to go to Moorpark with me grandfather – he was still working over there in them days – all the buggers over there when you were harvesting used to work the cider into 'un, dunnum!

Your mum wasn't very happy about that?

When we come back Mum used to sit on the stairs and cuss flashes, so she did reckon – well, I can't remember nothing about it!

What did your father do?

At the time he was working at the quarries I think, he worked for the council a bit, and he was in the Home Guard here. To start off with they used to ride up along the top road to get to Gare Hill, they had a hut in the wood up there where they used to go and guard. So he would go out and when they started they had a shot gun between five of them, and that belonged to a farmer. Well then in the end they ended up at the station here in Witham.

Do you remember the evacuees coming into Witham?

Oh yeah. In the beginning, 1940, there was loads of evacuees here then.

Did any live near you?

Right next door. They were two brothers, they came from Oxford, I think, in the first place. I went to school and that with them. And when the war was over they went back.

Right: Duncan's grandparents, seen here at 11 Rough Stubbs sometime in the nineteen-thirties. Duncan: *"The doorway's gone – it's a window in there now, I think. Me grandmother died a lot longer before than me grandfather did. He died up at Rough Stubbs."*

As a young child living here, where did you and your friends go and play?

Anywhere really, in the fields, anywhere, we'd go down the rivers and go fishing. We'd go and build camps out in the woods. You had to go and make your own enjoyment then. Basically, when we was up our end or the other end of the village we didn't go very far and there were just a few of you up there.

Did you like your teacher, Mrs Cunnington?

Yeah, she was alright. She'd always recognise you and go and speak to you. She used to come out [to Witham] on an early train and catch the four o'clock one back to Frome. She used to live up at Locks Hill [in Frome] at the time.

How different was it at Sexey's, the secondary school at Bruton?

It was a lot different because you had great big classes, I didn't know anybody else at the time. There was a fair few from Frome though that used to go, they had a boarding house then. We had season tickets to get there on the train. Also, we had to take our own grub down there – they didn't have their own canteen. I think it was the late nineteen-fifties before they had their own school meals down there. I left in 1951 so I must have been about sixteen I suppose, or a little older. Because down there you had to finish the year out, because my birthday is in February. If you went to school in Shepton you used to finish in the Easter, because one of the other ones who used to live up at Holt Cottages – his birthday was in October so he had to do another twelve months.

What was your first job?

Agricultural engineer. I stayed there my whole life and went and did my apprenticeship, cycling to Frome and back every day, with Archie Down and then I went up Warminster but it's now gone. I just went in and asked if they had a job and they said "Yeah" and in them days that was it. Basically when they started they only had three vans, most of the time to start off with we were in the workshop and then I finished my apprenticeship and had to do my National Service.

We joined up October 17th 1954, I think it was. They sent you the railway tickets to RAF Cardington [Bedford] where we was all kitted out and then we done our basic training at RAF West Kirby, Liverpool area. That was sort of October or November time and that was cold up there. Everything was froze. Then we was lucky, we went into training up in RAF Melksham so we went up there, we were lucky up there 'cos they had sessions where you could go and we was home for nearly a month before we had to go up because the other lot hadn't started yet. Then, you done your time, it were only three months up there, then we got where your permanent base is, RAF Wyton, and I thought – where the hell is that? We didn't know and nobody knew at Melksham. There was two of us there so we were basically together all the way through. It was lucky because the other bloke was a regular and was going back to Huntington.

What was it like at RAF Wyton?

It was Bomber Command, a big place. Well we was up there messing about with aeroplanes and they had too many regulars so some of us were given another job, I had a good cushy job doing next to nothing all the time. I suppose we were supposed to be mechanics, but some of the regulars got there before we did. I had a good time. I used to play football for one of the outside teams in the county league, well then you used to come home because you used to get so many free passes and you know, well if I came back from Huntington and to King's Cross and then to Paddington, I couldn't get home that night. But if I went to a place called St Ives up there, a bit more up the road, into Liverpool Street I could be home on the six o'clock train.

When I got back I was twenty-one. After we sort of done the apprenticeship and they had more vans we used to go out a lot, all over the place. Anywhere, really, we even did work up Kingston Seymour and Clevedon, we was going down there everyday. We used to go a long distance because they used to have another depot in Salisbury, Andover and Basingstoke, in summer we used to spend more time doing jobs up there than down here in Frome. We used to get called out at four in the morning – "Oh, me engine, oh, my milking machine don't work" – oh my God…then you used to come in for parts at ten or eleven o'clock at night when the season was on. So you had to put up with it. I used to do a lot of welding and all that stuff and that's what you used to do in the end. I couldn't work with all this electronics, it's ridiculous. All these tractors have stuff on them; you don't need it.

How many years did you do that for?

Until I retired. I didn't really retire, the bloke said – you can kick on if you want to – and I cut it down by a few days and then eventually packed it all in together.

Were there any jobs you didn't like doing?

Yeah, the muck spreaders, when they were full up with manure…

You were a keen footballer. Were you always a goalie?

When I was a kid I wasn't, I played in midfield. Then I went into goal and stuck to it then afterwards. I played for Witham to start off with, then I went off to Maiden Bradley, and then Butler and Tanner's in Frome. I left there for Wallington Westons where I broke me leg and packed it

Duncan's girlfriend Val sitting on his Triumph TR6 in 1961 after he fitted the sidecar. They married two years later

in. I collided and that was it. They had to screw it up, my right leg it was, I broke both bones. They put screws in there, it was like a self tapper, they took one out and the other is still in there.

Did you use your motorbike when the children were small?

It was after me national service that I joined the Frome and District Motorcycle Club. When I started there was just a little track in Asham woods until we cut it all out, it was right at the side of the road going past the lake. I spent most of my time out there. I used to do a lot of scramble courses around here but there aren't so many now. In the end I was getting too much of it and packed it in.

I had two BSAs and a Triumph TR6. My favourite was the TR6, it would do ninety-five down Highcroft with me brother on the back and there was more to come! Then I put a sidecar on it. Changed the engine sprocket to gear it down but it would still do eighty with the sidecar on. I would like to have kept it but Karen came along and I had to buy a van, you know. That bike would have been worth a lot of money now.

Brian Bullock,
Ruminant Nutritionist, 79

Brian Bullock at home in Frome, June 8th, 2015

There was a tremendous community of people that was working in agriculture but I suppose now, like every other village, that's all changed.

I was born at Rough Stubbs in 1936. The lady that lived in the end cottage was called Florrie Warren. She used to borrow the horse and cart from the local farmer; we used to go sticking. I can just remember – I must have only three or four years old – going up into the woods with her and my mother with the horse and cart and gather [sticks] and bring back so that we'd all have firewood to keep us warm.

We moved down into the main village in the early part of the war years. We lived in no. 51 which was just a cottage near to where the bungalows were built (in the garden). We had total and utter freedom, there was no traffic – you could play in the roads with footballs, we made a lot of our entertainment in those days with old bicycle wheels – there weren't very much to buy because of the war years. But it was wonderful having had the freedom of the countryside in our growing-up years. I think it set us in good stead for when we were older.

I suppose growing up in the village we were pretty safe from the disasters of the big cities [during the war]. I recall being in Frome with my mother shopping one Saturday morning. We was walking back to the station and there was all these soldiers coming out. They'd come back from Dunkirk. My God, what a sight, couldn't believe it; that sort of made you think. Some of them were injured and some were being carried, bandaged and dirty [but] they'd come back. Point of fact, one of 'em that we didn't notice was my uncle – a few weeks later he came and visited us – he was billeted to Marston House. I well recall seeing all the planes in the sky gathering for D-Day. I also have memories of the girl that was evacuated to us during the war arriving at our house with a little piece of cardboard wrapped around her neck to say what name she was. She stayed with us 'til after the war and she then went back to Dagenham, but she couldn't settle and she ran away and came back to live with us! She stayed, I mean people came down and it was all agreed and she stayed and worked in Frome, married there and then emigrated to Australia. She corresponded with my mother every month until mother died when she was eighty-six.

You mentioned about a bomb being dropped in the lake…

Farm workers were deferred (*i.e. had reserved occupations*) because of their type of employment. My grandfather Bill Compton and my uncle Bert North both worked at Manor Farm and they were fire watchers. It was in a November they were sent up to New House Farm which was derelict during the war. It was a very cold night so they lit the fire, the chimney caught fire and I think there was a German bomber coming back – it'd been damaged [so] he had to unload his bombs – whether he saw the fire or not he dropped the bomb and it knocked the end of the lake out at the Hermitage. I don't think they were the flavour of the month because they lost the fish! But I think that story's been told on many occasions.

What was the school like?

Very spartan you know, certainly in the winter months! We all used to go armed with stick to keep us warm and coal was on ration – it was a bit of a barn of a place and only one fire and one room so it wasn't exactly that comfortable. But I don't think it bothered us that much. And then in the autumn of each year we were all paid so much to gather in the haws or hips, rather, to make rosehip syrup and we used to take those to school and they were collected and sent off somewhere to make the rosehip syrup. So it was, you know, people were pretty much involved and the whole of the village sort of centred around, really I suppose, the school and the church.

How was Mrs Cunnington as a teacher?

She was very fair, she was very firm, and it wasn't 'til after I left school that I wished I'd tried a bit harder. (*laughs*) And I told her on many occasions!

So later you went to school in Shepton – how long were you there for?

Until just before I was fifteen. We took the train each day and I remember in the Witham winter of forty-seven which was a very, very cold winter (the miners were on strike), they only had enough coal to keep the steam trains going and there was very little heat to come into the carriage. I well remember going down through the cutting into Doulting – the train drove straight into a snow drift and they was stopped the whole of the day until we were dug out at night.

You were involved with the church choir...

Yes, I think it was about 1947 we had a change of vicars. The Reverend Dunn, he died and then we had a Reverend Bawtree-Williams who was ordained and became minister at Witham church. He was a doctor of music and he had been a minister in Africa. He had diabetes so he wasn't eligible to go into the war, so he took over the cathedral choir in Wells and then after the war he came to Witham and brought music to the village – and course all us young lads and lasses were drawn into the choir to sing and they suddenly realised I had an exceptionally good voice and it started my interest in music. Diabetes affected his eyesight; he was going blind. Through that he started a harvest festival service for the blind which was broadcast live from Witham by the BBC on the first Monday in October *(1956, on the BBC Home Service at three o'clock, between 'For the Schools' and 'Angel Pavement' by J.B. Priestley)*. The church was all decorated with strong smelling flowers and plants and herbs and things so the blind people could feel a part of it.

By now my voice had broken, I was singing tenor and I had to go down [to the church] because they had to fix the mics up to make sure they were in the right place before they went live. Cables running to the railway station for transmission; Dudley Savage playing the organ! There was about nine hundred and fifty people eligible to come to that service from North East Somerset. As I got to the church, buses were unloading. Not all of them were blind – some were partially sighted. I was going to sing this solo and obviously a bit concerned about it because if I made a mistake it would of been [heard] worldwide. But it was this young girl, totally and utterly blind, similar age to myself, smiling and quite happy… they asked me to help her up the steps into the church.

She gave me a tremendous boost of confidence! I thought, well, gosh, what am I worried about? I'm not blind, I've got everything, so I was able to sing and not worry at all about it. I've never, ever seen her from that day to this. As far as I understand there are recordings of those services in the BBC archives. Yes, they were broadcast. I definitely know it was broadcast worldwide because Humphrey Jowett what took over the farms, Lower West Barn and Higher West Barn farms, eventually had Manor as well, he were still in Australia then and heard it there.

My first job, in fact my only job in Witham was at Tynemead Farm. They was very, very short of labour and though I'd done my exams at school, I was able to leave and my [fifteenth] birthday wasn't until the February, but I never went back to school after Christmas. So I started on the farm and in those days there was a mixture of horses and tractors and by the time I was sixteen I took over milking the herd of cows and I milked the herd until I was about twenty-six or seven.

It was rather a long day. We started half past five every day so that in fact were it summer or winter we could have the milking machines operating by six o'clock, mainly because we wanted the milk into the dairy because my sister was the cheese-maker. We needed it to be there at a regular time – certainly so that they could start making cheese by nine o'clock in the morning. Then we started milking again at four o'clock and would probably be finished by six, or half past, so the days were rather long. All the attendant problems that you have with dairies had to be seen to during the day, as well as field work and making the feed for the winter [too]. So every day was at least a ten hour day and in them early days we only got a half day a week off and what[ever] time we had between milkings on Sundays so we worked rather long hours.

And my first pay packet was fifty-two [shillings] and sixpence a week for sixty hours! Yes, we got paid in cash and not always on time because the farmer was always busy. He said "Well, I paid you last week, you ought to have a bit left," but we had to pay me mother…so, he always paid us and we never, ever went without and I always remember when I had my first five pound note – my wages came to four pound nineteen and something and I had to bring back a few pence to make it up!

Opposite: Witham Church Choir, pictured in church one Christmas during the mid nineteen-fifties. Above: 1. Gill Thane, 2. Mr Thane, 3. Sue May, 4. Mr Cunnington, 5. Sandra Wheeler, 6. Patsy Naylor, 7. Mrs. Thane, 8. Jimmy May, 9. Peter Cary, 10. Linda Naylor, 11. Catherine Cox, 12. Anthony Jackson, 13. Jackie White, 14. Brian Bullock, 15. Arthur Cox, 16. Beryl Bullock, 17. Michael Kerslake, 18. Val Naylor, 19. Harry Wheeler, 20. Anna Thane, 21. Reverend Bawtree-Williams

How many cows did you have to milk?

Well, we were rather a big herd in those days. Ayrshires was the cattle we had because [their] quality of milk, in particular the protein side of the milk was very, very good for making cheese. We always tried to keep milking somewhere about eighty cows, we milked them in the winter in the stalls and in the summer we milked them in the bail.

Were you the only herdsman?

No – I always had someone to help me, you know, the lad from the village generally speaking and there was boys that came down from London, boys who actually wanted to work on the farm and the land. There was some good boys came from there and they always had one of those. That helped me.

Tell me how the cheese making was done.

The milk was tipped into a tank, then heated and rennet and things were added and then it had to be scalded and brought to a temp – to a stage where they could drain the whey off and then take the curd out, put it into tubs, press it and then take them out again the next day. Eventually they went into a cheese store and they stayed up there for three or four months. Good cheddar cheese, really you don't ever start eating much until after six months.

Was that sold locally or was it put on the train?

It was collected and taken to Crump and Way in Wells. They used to send a cheese tester to grade the cheeses, then we'd load up out of the chute onto the lorry. They would average somewhere around fifty pound in weight, made in truckles, all Cheddar. Occasionally they'd have a session of making Caerphilly. They were taken down – and they're still going – to Barber's of Ditcheat who dealt with them and then they were taken to South Wales – primarily for the miners' lunchboxes. Of course the cheeses that you made for certain shows and things, you selected the cheese and you knew what day the show was likely to be and therefore you made the cheese accordingly. My sister, she was a very good cheese maker and she took third prize in the London Dairy Show one year from making Caerphilly cheese.

And you did some work for the local blacksmith…

Where we lived in Witham, behind us was Mr Savin who was the local blacksmith and had been for many, many years [doing] many jobs around Witham, both timber and metal work. I often used to go down in spare time if I had a day off and blow the furnace for him, help him shoe horses and help him put band steels onto cart wheels – it was a very,

very interesting thing to watch him do. He was a lovely old boy and he eventually gave up and I had the job of cleaning out the blacksmiths before they sold up. If you come down the hill into Witham and if you go down the track to Tynemead Farm, instead of going on down [to the farm] you turn right again – that was the blacksmith's shop. It's now a house, and such for sale I see.

I understand that your father worked on the railway.

Yes, the railway was a very important part of Witham life. It was the junction for the line that came in from Wells, which was always called the 'Cheddar Valley.' In those days there were the station master, the signalman and the ganger, those were the three people that actually worked together. My father was the ganger. He had a gang of about six blokes that used to work with him *(pause)* so long as I can remember. Every day he'd set the blokes going, then walk his length from the boundary in Witham which he looked out to, right to Frome North. His job to make sure that the line was in good order and in good repair. Knock the keys in *(a wooden block between the rail and the 'chair')*. He didn't like the idea of continuous welded rail.

You talked about the line buckling…

It was in June. It was a very, very hot June. When my father walked the length to Frome North, one way and back the other, he noticed coming into Witham station the line had buckled with the heat. An emergency! You'd put down a series of detonators on [the line], three that you'd put down that would stop the train. The Cornish Riviera Express ran through Witham somewhere approaching half-past twelve everyday and he stopped it coming in – had it of gone over the buckled line it may well have been derailed. If you think of the consequences as a train coming off on that bank at the speed…it doesn't bear thought. They used to hurtle in there!

By then the railway had been nationalised and was British Rail – you know, the next day it was heck of a lot of people there *(pause)* looking at the whole thing. The pressure they put on him. It destroyed my father. The fact it had happened on his length. He had a lot of pride in the job; he never really got over it. It was the late fifties then. He retired from the railway as an invalid and then we managed to move him into Frome and he got a little part-time job going down early in the morning to the Post Office. He loved it down there!

He was probably an asthmatic as a boy; his mother was a midwife but she died when he was fourteen or fifteen. My grandfather was left with three boys and my father was the youngest. So he went wild… It was in the late twenties, in the depression, when it was difficult to get work and men used to go down on a Friday to see if they could get work on the railway. They tried to elbow one another, it was pretty tough. And eventually to get shot of him the railway gave him a job, sent him in to working in the Severn Tunnel, in the fumes there. It destroyed his chest. And of course he smoked, as they all did in the war… He died in 1970; he was sixty-four.

You weren't tempted to go and work on the railways?

Not at all, no, no.

You became a manager for three farms?

Mr Jakins (that was my boss at Tynemead), he sold up and the new people came in. Then the manager left and the owner Harrison Cripps gave me the job of running all three farms – Tynemead Farm, Walk Farm and Moorleaze. It was a huge job and in those days very difficult. We never had the machinery that they got today to manage these things and I probably realised that farm management really, at the end of the day, wasn't for me – and having been in agriculture ever since I realised that no farm manager ever lasts more than five years, so I think I got out in time. I've traded with so many since! Well, I left Tynemead, it'll be fifty years come this October, I worked in contract milking, this firm had dairies around the country and I ran those. Eventually I migrated back into the feed industry...animal feeds. Right the way through. Until a month ago. I've just retired – at seventy-nine! I thoroughly enjoyed it so it really wan't a chore. I still miss it but I feel that it's time to move on, really. Super chap taking over from me, I told him "Play everything straight, it's the only way. If anything's wrong, put your hand up – don't let it fester, put it right." Farming was the main thing in Witham – I mean the people at the pub, they had cows – the people at the Manor Farm, they had cows, through the whole village all the farms were dairy farms, and so there was a tremendous community of people that was working in agriculture. But I suppose now, like every other village, that's all changed.

Did your father rent no. 51?

Yes. He was a tenant. The rent was five shillings a week *(the 1951 auction particulars state for no. 51: 'Let to Mr. S. Bullock at £13, 0s. 0d. per annum payable half-yearly at Lady Day and Michaelmas)*. I think the cottage was sold for one hundred and seventy quid. Why didn't we buy it? Billy Longman bought it. He had an interest in the land, whereas Mr Jakins had an interest in the business. He was a forward seeing man.

My grandfather was Bill Compton – quite a character. When he retired – he stayed on at Manor, that's when the Jowetts bought the Manor Farm, he stayed on part-time for them. And Humphrey Jowett's father-in-law was chairman of Cunards *(Sir Basil Smallpeice, chair of Cunard Line from 1965 to 1972)*. He used to come down in this Rolls-Royce and take me gran'father out. He absolutely idolised my gran'father's simple life. You wouldn't believe it. He took 'im down there [to Southampton] onto the Queen something or other *(QE2, maiden voyage in May 1969)*, for lunch. Wearing a pair of old slip-on shoes!

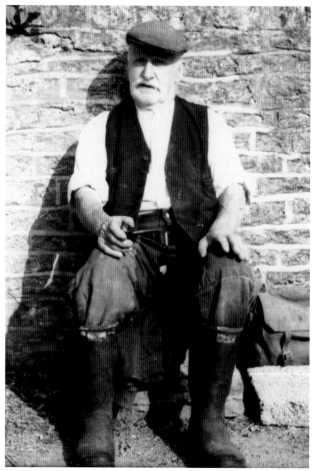

Gramp Compton, with his pipe, wellies, belt and army surplus bag

Brian Bullock: *"He used to come on the back of me old bike — he was my first pillion passenger — I don't know whether I was old for my age or whether he was young for his but we din't seem too much apart in our age! Quite a character."*

Melvyn Walton: *"He died in his garden. Jimmy May and Cliff Stevens discovered him there. What a way to go!"*

Melvyn Walton, Railwayman, 71

Music is my first love – except for the wife

I'm Melvyn Walton.
Back in the day I used to live
at 49 Witham Friary with
my granddad who was
known as Gramp
to everyone in the village.
I now live in Frome.

What memories do you have of school life in the village?

Well, I can visualise the short trousers. At meal times we had rice pudding with jam and I can remember walking home with my mum when she remarked about the jam which had spilt on my trousers. In the school we had the old type desks with the lift-up lids and the ink wells; the heating was from a cylindrical stove which didn't work very well. They were good, but cold days! We were a close-knit family within the school. Miss Hunt, our teacher at the time, was strict but good – she must have been – when the eleven-plus exams were taken, three of us passed; myself, Maurice Cox and Stella Cox. After passing, Stella had first entry into Sunny Hill School in Bruton, Maurice [Stella's cousin] and I had to take an entry exam at Sexey's School in Bruton, but having failed that we moved to St John's in Frome.

What were your favourite lessons at school?

Music and spelling and geography. Spelling I do like. Music is my first love – except for the wife.

When you were a youngster you joined the choir…

I joined as a chorister when I was about five or six – we used to have practice on a Thursday evening. It was Evensong on a Sunday, but I used to like singing at the festivals. I had a good time within the church choir and I was made head boy. I used to lead the choir into the church at festivals and Christmas and would sing a solo along with my cousin Brian Bullock. Good King Wenceslas: I would sing the part of the page boy and Brian sang the part of the king – I would then lead us out singing a solo. I had an enjoyable time – I used to love singing. In them days the church was shunned to a certain degree, but it always had its followers.

What did you used to get up to as a child?

We used to spend a lot of time in this hollow tree which was in the field opposite the vicarage – we used to climb up there and swing about before jumping off. We wandered across the fields and made our own things – we even had trolleys that we made from pram wheels; they were like go-karts and we used to go up Vicarage Hill and ride down and around the corner. Some of us would fall off down the track way… it was good fun and during the winter out opposite Littlewoods, a big hole – I can't remember now what it was called – but during the winter a gang of us would get a big sheet of galvanised and bend the end up and slid down the snow. That was good fun. I have no idea how deep that was, but maybe up to forty feet. During the summer we used to go off up into the woods and play hide and seek; two or three would stay by the church while half a dozen would go up to the woods and hide. Opposite the pub we used to get a lot of water, during the winter that would freeze over and we'd go with torches and skate with our bikes over the ice. It was good.

Health and safety wouldn't let us do it now – never ever! I can remember in 1953, coronation year, there was a big fete. I know we had a big marquee, lots of bunting, balloons, and those sorts of things. We were so wrapped up with the fancy dress that we had to keep ourselves in order. The village did celebrate the coronation, but I don't think people would do it today. It was outside of the pub in the big field there. It was fancy dress and skittles – everything associated with a village fete. Fancy dress was the thing. Myself and my cousin Beryl Bullock were entered into the fete as the Bisto kids – 'Ahhh, Bisto…' Costumes were made by my mother and Maggie Bullock; Beryl's mother. We won the competition!

Melvyn, tell us about the first jobs that you did.

My first job was at Tynemead farm with Leo Jakins who was the farmer at the time. He used to help me and I used to go over after school and on weekends – all this was for 2/6 a week (*note to younger readers: equivalent to 12½ pence*). It was a youngsters' thing I suppose, I tormented Brian and different things like that. We used to race up and down the cow stalls near the milk churns which were filled. I didn't win many times. Another I can remember: I finished washing up the dairy utensils and so started to torment Brian who then decided to put me into the steam chest, shutting the door. It was a punishment but it was funny. At Christmas we used to have to pluck the geese for Farmer Jakins. Brian and Barry Baker used to cover me in grease and feathers before putting me in a sugar beet sack and hanging me up – leaving me for a couple of hours before coming back and chucking water on me. They got me out eventually, but it was all good fun. We enjoyed tormenting each other; calling each other names, etc. I used to call Brian 'Ogsworth' – still do whenever I see him! I then got a job at Moorpark farm with Ren Stevens. He took me on when I left school in and I was with him for three years. I didn't enjoy it as I was the only employee there: it was a family concern and I always wanted to work on the railway. The railway was my ambition. I wanted to be a signal man. I used to spend time in Witham signal box with my neighbour Bob Cruse and eventually got a job at Cranmore signal box in 1960. First I went for an interview with Inspector Shepherd at Yatton and then the Bristol office – they asked me questions about the rules and regulations for running a signal box.

I could tell them everything, along with the bell-codes [for signalling trains], and so they said: "Well, we've got to give you the job."

"Why?" I asked.

"Because you know so much," they said, "congratulations!"

At eighteen I was the youngest signalman for British Railways in the Western Region which I thought was very good. I couldn't be a signal-man on the mainline until I was twenty-one so I moved to the 'P Way' (*Permanent Way, i.e. the track maintenance gang*) with Fred Warren the ganger – I cycled up the path by the side of the track from Witham to Cranmore to book on every morning with that gang!

After that I spent another year around the permanent way in Witham before leaving for Frome. A job came up as a delivery driver so I applied for that and got it – but I couldn't drive! So courtesy of British Rail I learnt to drive at Taplow, in February 1963. I did pass my test and spent six months delivering parcels. Funnily enough, Witham was a part of my delivery area so I did come back delivering parcels.

Melvyn Walton at home. Frome, June 8th, 2015

Do you look back with affection on the village?

Sometimes. Although I often wish I had stayed; things have changed so I'm glad to have left. If it's any good for the village I don't know. The village does have fond memories for me.

Robert Ludgate, Engineer, 74

I was a farmer's boy. I was steeped in shite. Loved it. I enjoyed the nitty-gritty country farmer side but at the same time I always had this bent for aircraft and technical things…

Robert Ludgate was recorded on the 9th of January 2012 at 7 Rough Stubbs, Witham. Beneath that taciturn demeanour lies a charming man. He keeps his own counsel even today at his house in Rough Stubbs. His life has followed several twists and turns, and he is now paraplegic after a motorcycle accident in 2007. Here he reflects on past days…

Above: Robert aged thirteen and a half in 1953

Opposite: Robert's mother, Christina Bowles was born in 1897 at Lower Slaughter, Gloucestershire. This beautiful study made by the local studio in Cirencester, *'Patronised by Royalty'* embossed on the print, pictures her at the age of 26. She married Howard, Robert's father three years later

My father was the stationmaster at Pill, near the outskirts of Bristol. I was part of a family of four or five – three other brothers and an elder sister. My mum was pretty poorly; I moved down here before she died – sent down here to live with my aunt and uncle [at Holt Farm]. My father decided to do that. It must have been 1950? It was not uncommon [for families to be split up then]; we had two or three maiden aunts in the family. The boys were farmed out to them – one went to a primary teacher at Fairford, the other was a farmer's wife in Edington. Chris went to Fairford: Edward to Edington.

You saw your father often?

No. When I was at the farm I remember him coming down once. He died in 1967.

Did you go back for his funeral?

No. I don't remember where I was, very vague, it wasn't a big thing. I don't know whether the rest of the family went, I think my oldest brother and sister, and John were there; whether Edward went or not I don't know. So I missed all the family funerals.

Your aunt was Alice, your mother's sister?

Yes. She was the second wife of Fred Nicholls. He [already] had four kids, three boys and one girl: Len, Philip, Bernard, and Edna. She got this post at Wanstrow primary school and got to the Nicholls from there. At that time there would have been three of the [Nicholls] boys, possibly the eldest girl all at once at school together. I think they used to run the King William and the Post Office and haulage on the side. That was when uncle Fred's first wife died and then my aunt married him shortly after. Whether they had any land over there I'm not sure; I think he used to do a bit of haulage then they moved from Wanstrow pre-war to rent Holt Farm off the Duke.

When I came here to live the youngest son, Len, was early twenties. I moved to Holt Farm. Len was more or less running the farm then – Fred must've been late sixties. Len was much older than me – I didn't really move into a family. Until Len got married in the middle fifties, I was up there.

I failed my eleven plus; it was a big thing then. I went to Frome school [Oakfield]. The normal place to go from Witham was Shepton. But Oakfield Secondary Modern as it was then that had quite a good reputation so my aunt was keen to get me in there. Of my contemporaries down at Witham: Roger Gale, Gordon Stevens, Derek White – I think Gordon and Roger passed their eleven-plus and went to Sexey's, the others went to Shepton. We all caught the train to school from Witham and [I used to] leg it across town every morning to Oakfield. I had a season ticket – applied to the council for that, didn't have to buy it at the station. I'd cycle down in the morning. It was some poxy diesel [to Frome]. There were three girls who must've be late teens who were on the train; Keeper Day's daughter, Anne? And Cynthia Miles from Witham Hall farm. Only saw them in the morning and in the evening it was a Hall [steam locomotive] or something bigger. A big job, going all the way to Weymouth! I pushbiked from Witham station back up to Holt Farm.

What livestock was on the farm?

Aside from the dairy herd there were chickens, we kept pigs at one time; not too many. I remember when one had a litter and I bullied my uncle into selling me one – so he sold me this piglet – less than a week later it died. It was obvious that it would die; he was grinning because he'd sold me a dud! My aunt took pity on me and said I should ask for my ten bob back. That was my only foray into livestock… They always used to keep horses. My uncle was keen on horses, he kept a cob one time. Len used to ride that a bit and then I took to ride that a bit and then he bought a brood mare. Mary [Len's wife] was keen on horses. But [although] they were more interested in the heavy horse, my uncle took a fancy to this racehorse, a broken-down old nag.

I don't know if ever they had working horses, I'm not sure. When I arrived it was tractors. I was a farmer's boy. I was steeped in shite. I was steeped in horseshit and cowshit. Ah, love it. Loved it. It's funny, I enjoyed the nitty-gritty country farmer side but at the same time I always had this bent for aircraft and technical things, really into that.

Summer, 1950. Haymaking in Mill Ground, Holt Farm, looking northeast towards Rough Stubbs and Witham village.
From left: Bert Nicholls, Anne (Irish Land Girl), Alf Baker, Harry Proctor, Wilf Wheeler, Robert Ludgate & Fred Nicholls

But the whole business of living on a farm at that time. Most kids were farmer's sons or farm workers' sons. Just different stuff that you don't experience now or know about much, like killing badgers. I forget the first one we got, dug him out from somewhere: always remember going out to Brewham one day, one Sunday morning, dug a badger, killed him there. I brought him back, strung him up by the sawbench behind Holt Farm and skinned it and sent off this pelt to a place up in Wisbech. I got some money for it! Loved it.

Corner them in the sett. I suppose set the dogs in there, anybody's terriers that were going and the gathering reshuffles and big sticks get digging; dig down till you see him, dig down into the sett. By that time you're close enough to kill him beginning with a shovel. Over the head with a shovel.

And then there was fox hunting because one of these horses were at Holt Farm. I used to go fox hunting quite a few times – I was crazy about it, South and West Wilts [Hunt]. I was fourteen or thirteen, I'd learnt to ride a horse. By then, I got treated pretty well really; the eldest son [of Fred] Bernard Nicholls, his daughter was taking riding lessons up near Hindon. I used to go up with them to take riding lessons. They ran the mill at Kilmington, the sawmills there. His daughter was a bit younger than me. I cycled out Kilmington.

I was mad keen on horses for while and that died away. Going to different places; we just went hunting. Didn't dwell on the moral or ethical aspects of it then, just if you were fortunate enough to have a horse to do it. Similar to killing badgers and digging foxes. At that time back in the fifties, every farmer used to take it for granted that the hunt would cross his land; might even feel aggrieved if they didn't come across! And guns: guns everywhere then. When I went up to the farm first there was a gun rack in the back kitchen – a normal kitchen like a domestic kitchen. There were at least two shotguns, a four-ten and a twelve bore; a rifle up there as well. Rifle came back from the war, a Mauser .22 which we used to shoot. That was good. Everybody had shotguns. You never thought about safety with guns at all,

never thought the barrel should be broken before you waved it around. A normal thing; we never thought about these things at all. Never went wrong exactly, but I remember one time when we used to grow corn in at Wood Ground, a triangular five or six acre ground up by Fry's Wood; then Len would come to thrash [it]; that old thrasher would be going, chopping off the sheaves around. Get right to the end, all the rabbits in there would make a break for it, there would be four or five guns around there. People would be banging off left, right and centre, and I remember there was my uncle Fred, probably Len and Keeper Day, the gamekeeper for the Duke's estate. who lived up the road [at 1 or 2 Witham Friary]. And my uncle Fred's brother Reuben, a kind of beery chap from Wanstrow; they were all taking the piss out of Reuben at the end when we were sat around, because Ted Day said he was picking a pellet out of his leg – they said that was one of Reuben's when he had a stray shot! Not too sure which direction he was shooting! It was all sort of haphazard. No one was ever badly injured; a bit of a laugh and a smirk, saying "Yeah, one of your bloody pellets in my leg, Reuben – that's bloody Reuben!"

The best fox we dug out was opposite Miles's farm, Witham Hall Farm. A rick they had between the farm and the railway line. Fox was burrowed there, had got into there, made a den at the top of the rick. Definitely a fox was in there. We got in there one day – must've been a weekend when we did – killing on the Sunday.

We had big hay knives, then cut them into the rick. We got in there. I always remember that was great, exciting time. We had big hay knives, then sliced them down into the rick, cutting out great wedges of hay; got the fox out. Someone got close enough to fox then shot. And for quite a time after that, well, as long as a rick was standing yet, say eighteen months, I used to go backwards and forwards to school on the train, I'd look across there and see a nice shaped rick with a big hole on top of it opposite Miles's. It wasn't in the side of the base. It was right in the top of the rick where we'd cut it.

A landmark! Come along West Woodlands, past the copses, under Bunns Lane bridge, see Witham Hall Farm on the right and the rick with a big piece cut, a big chunk cut out of the top. Oh yes, there used to be a fox in there! I'll always remember that.

Above: Holt farm, early fifties. Rob's Aunt Alice and Uncle Fred with their Austin 16
Opposite: Having aisled up the stooks, Rob's Uncle Fred (right) and Keeper Day get the guns out for the rabbits during harvest

Who drove the tractor on the farm?

Len or the farmworker Harry Proctor. Harry went to work on the railway afterwards, he was in the office at Witham in the station. In my early teens he would have been in the office. We used to collect things from Witham station, we went to the yard to load sugarbeet pulp, load that on…from the sidings this side of the line. The down yard. It never ceases to surprise me when I think about it: how something as substantial as the station house, the ticket office, the bridge over the line, the sidings and the sep-arate platform for Yatton, how it can all have been obliterated? I was away in the RAF and the station shut. I don't remember anything about it. It's odd – it didn't happen overnight. I thought I would have seen some signs of debris or rubbish. When I think how substantial it was! There was a waiting room on the other side of the line as well. I vaguely remember the stationmaster knew of my father, which I suppose is normal for a big organisation like that. About the only thing that is left is the sidings? No signal box. Not since 1984.

What became of your aunt and uncle?

They carried on at the farm until 1970 when my uncle died. My aunt moved then from Holt Farm to Hermitage Lodge. Len carried on up the farm. At that time it was Len, Mary and their two boys, Fred and Jess. They were all up at the Hermitage [Lodge], so it was a big swap over.

They must have bought this house, 7 Rough Stubbs?

She [my aunt] bought this with her own money.

So she had enough money to buy this house in the fifties?

Say 'enough money' but it was all scrimp and save, a bit here and a bit there. It was a massive sum to get together for her to buy this, even though it was derelict. It was the one thing she had to be sure of in later life. She bought this as barely a two-up, two-down with a pantry on the back, a water boiler stuck in the corner. I don't think it even had a proper toilet. Flo and Annie Warren, they existed quite happily sat around the stove. And the main sink was only one cold water pipe in a sink stuck in the front room. Which wasn't uncommon for any rural cottage, but looking back now, you think: God, that was a bit basic – but that's what I used to have. So, there was one big room with a partition across there and the same upstairs; one largish bedroom and the landing. And this [kitchen] was a lean-to linked on the back bit, less depth than it is now. The extension increased the depth and put two dormer bedrooms above and the proper toilet and everything. She moved down here when I finished renovating it in about '76. Whilst I was still travelling up to Reading! I was doing shiftwork up there and I used to come backwards and forwards. My aunt died a year after she moved down here. She was seventy-seven. I went to her funeral down at the village here. She's in Witham churchyard. Alice Emily Nicholls. 1900 to 1977. The house was made over to me so then I stayed here. I got this job in Monmouth and I covered five or six different sites; major computer installations over the south-west. There was no such thing as laptops or desktops. It was just a room with 'our computer' – that sort of thing. So it was very interesting: various places – Southampton, Swindon, Cardiff, South Wales coast. It was alright. I did that for as long as the firm was going back in the early eighties. My firm was taken over. I was made redundant.

Tell me about the Witham football team.

I was pretty pally with Marcus Powell at Upper Holt Farm. We used to go and play five-a-side and we used to work on the farm in the village. It was different; a lot more young chaps around in the late seventies. We started off by playing with his mate Dave Cox, they played for Brewham, so I said "Brewham – any chance of a game with them?" "Yes, he said, they're always short" – couple of times we played for Brewham. It was so poor, would turn up sometimes there'd be only about five or six – and three of them would be from Witham: me, Marcus and Dave! So we said "This is a bloody joke, we'll start our own team in Witham," which is what we did. Our first season was 1979. I think the last secretary was Dick Kerslake, used to live at Kerry Croft, Dick and Betty. Dick used to work on the railway. He ran the football team. Used to live where Hazel & Brian Hurle live now. His lot packed up in the middle to late sixties, the team was well defunct – there were no goalposts. I don't know where their pitch was.

Our first pitch was up at Moorleaze. As you go up the Upton Noble road before Moorleaze, about halfway up on the left by the little stile across a field by a gateway, which is a wood now. We had that for three seasons. Then that was sold to Brian Stevens, or maybe he rented it off Clive Young. When Brian rented the field he said "I want you off," and we saw Ron Ham and got Hammy's field down behind where New Friary cottages are now. It ran east-west; the eastern end was almost in line with the end of Kerry Croft gardens. We almost went up to the back of the gardens with the goalposts. We played there for quite a few years.

Photo opposite: Witham Friary Football Team, 1979-80
Back row, left to right: Richard Toton, Danny Sheppard, Marcus Powell, John Gould, Dave Cox, Jeremy Gould
Front row, left to right: Robert Ludgate, Phil Stevens, Geoff Sheppard, Ian Farmer, Brian Burdon, Mark Stringer, Pete Oakes, Ronnie Garrick (manager)

Rob joined the RAF as a radio fitter direct from school in 1955. He transferred to aircrew in 1963, training as a wireless operator at the Air Electronics School in RAF Topcliffe before being stationed at RAF Ballykelly in 204 Squadron. There he flew in Avro Shackletons, the standard maritime aircraft for Coastal Command at the time. The squadron undertook various detachments and here Rob is pictured in Majunga during their detachment to Madagascar in 1967, supporting the UN blockage of Rhodesia by undertaking reconnaisance flights over the Beira Straits after Ian Smith declared UDI in November 1965

Who was in the team then?

Lovely chaps. Geoff Shepherd, John Gould, Dave Cox was a centre forward, Phil Stevens, Danny Shepherd, if we could get him; me, Marcus: who else? There must have been someone else. Young Jeremy, Jeremy Gould. He used to come on and then I used to go off because I was getting past it. Rich Toton from Wanstrow, couple of lads, another one Gary, I forget his name; come over from Wanstrow. Marcus by now was working for Cuprinol in Frome, a couple of blokes from there who were handy players who came out. My prime consideration was that the players should be from Witham; two-thirds [of the team] were Witham residents and the other third were from outside because they would be mates with whoever – mates of Marcus's usually. [We] didn't go and ask people who were unknown to the team, or anything at all, it was usually a more chummy basis 'cause that was the whole ethos of the village team to start with. I gave up in the early eighties and then I think Dave Cox's son managed for while. It almost petered out, but then Richard Gould took it up again. I think when he got it going again their home pitch was in Gypsy Lane, Frome. It wasn't 'til sometime later they got the pitch down here. [By then] it was difficult to get any farmer to allow you to use their land. Also, the regulations they weren't quite so lax as when we were started. You didn't have to bother too much with changing rooms or showers or anything like that. In fact, you were considered quite effete if you wanted a shower after the game. You just pulled your trousers on over your muddy knees and went down the pub. For Chrissakes, a shower? Who are you?

And the pub…

I never really went in the pub much. I do remember being at the head of the fancy dress parade playing The Archers theme tune on my violin, in fifty-two or three. But then I didn't really go down there until I started to play football and it was still very much as it always had been; no toilets or anything, go across the yard to the slates out in the back there. Yes, as you go around the opening where Pete [Douel] keeps his Volkswagens and stuff now. Just to the right there was some galvanised tin and in there was a big slate stood up, to piss against. It ran down into some sort of gutter. If you stood back far enough. That was the toilets. You never bothered to do any other ablutions down there if you had any sense. Of course, women would have to ask Jean to use her toilet in the pub. But they always had two fires on, that was very jolly, before bar billiards, before the one-armed bandit.

That's all I remember. Thanks for the beer. I'll get all my jobs done now.

Rob makes a point whilst preparing his vegetables, August 4th, 2015

Gordon Stevens gives the photographer an old-fashioned look. Wincanton, April 17th, 2015

Gordon Stevens, Farmer, 73

There's history there in the field names: Dirtymead, across here you've got Little Thanks - Great Watermead, that speaks for itself – Oat Close, bit of good ground there; you need good ground to grow oats on.

Gordon was born in Witham in 1940 and lived at Gibbons Farm until he married in 1961, when he moved to 3 Holt Cottages. Swapping houses with his parents in 1973, he returned to Gibbons until he quit farming and sold the farm in 2002. Now retired, he and his wife Bess live in Wincanton.

I can remember your mother telling me her family came from Sea Mills.

Well, originally they were farming at Shirehampton, and then they got pushed out of there by the carbon black factory because all the fields turned black with soot. Then they went to Lawrence Weston and then he came down to Witham about 1934 and took the tenancy of Gibbons. Father met mother from Gibbons and they got married in thirty-eight, I think, he took over the tenancy at Gibbons in 1939, just over a month away from war. One hundred and ninety acres, £200 per annum. So that's where I arrived in due course – the rest as they say is history!

What about your father's family – were they local?

They come up from Wedmore. Father's uncle, he came up to Little West Barn Farm, across the railway line, what date I don't know but he came up first. And my grandfather Charles Stevens came with his family to Moorpark; Father went to Witham school for a time as his name was still carved in a desk down there when I was there! Well then…mother met father and then his brother, well his eldest brother was farmin' at Maiden Bradley – my cousins are still there now – his sister married a William Green that farmed at Baycliffe *(a mile towards Longbridge Deverill from Bradley)* and grandfather bought some land down Witham that the Gartells had been farming from Manor Farm and built Homemead Farm for Donald.

We saw in the photo that Gibbons was completely mixed farming…

Gibbons – I don't think that our family was involved in it at all, but if you go back to around 1860 or thereabouts and you look on some of the old maps then, Gibbons farmhouse was only half the size that it was when we were there – I mean if you go down there now it's something else again, but there was another, bigger farm two fields further down. Spencer's. That was demolished; the stone was used, and timber, was used to make Gibbons bigger and also equip it for cheesemaking. The attic floors were reinforced and there was a lift put up outside; a door put in the gable end, and you put your cheeses on the platform, wound the handle and took 'em in at the top, for maturin' an' that. I don't think my maternal grandfather was involved in that, I never saw cheese made there but it would've been; all the equipment was there in the attic when I was a kid, growing up, you know, we used to mess around with the curd grinder but you had to make sure you didn't put your fingers in there! And the big cheese vat was about that deep *(gestures to about four feet wide)*, made of iron and would be four or five feet in diameter – we would get that upright and get inside and roll along in it just like a hamster!

"That's mother's mother, Gladys Gingell at Gibbons Farm in 1935. Hens, pigs, cattle!"

There had been a structure at Gibbons but it wasn't originally a farm?

It was more like a hunting lodge, I would've thought, a keeper's lodge or somethin' like that size. It was just…well as you go down to Gibbons now you see the front of the house, but the rear was added – you can tell if you go in the house and look – the beams in here [the front] were adzed and edged with plaster, the beams in this part [the rear] were sawn, [reclamation] added from Spencer's. If you go in the back door and go to your left you go into what was the old dairy, and that's an oak door, studded oak door, obviously at one time an outside door, and it's got at the top a vee-shaped wedge, a rathole, so that end was once that end *(points to floor)*. Upstairs in one room there were two lots of floorboards. One went one way and were about yea wide; and the other boards went the other way and they were about that wide, and they had nail holes but no nails

116

in them; yeah, they had nails down but they also had holes – they'd been reused. I don't know how much of it have now survived. At one time you could walk through Gibbons farmhouse and read it as a history book. How much you still can I don't know cos there's been a lot of changes there.

So the farm as you remember it as a child – there was a water supply?

Yes, the piped water was in then – best as I can remember, the pipe come into the house; there was a Belfast sink with a single cold tap running into it. And that was one of the reasons why my grandmother agreed to come to Gibbons Farm, because it had a piped water supply. Where they'd been before the water had to be fetched from a well. That was a major plus as far as she was concerned! Up to about 1947, up 'til then it was a working farm, cows were milked there, the milk went from there. Father always had pigs about. Mother, she had a lot, well, for those times a lot of hens. They were producing eggs, they used to go over to a packing station at Wanstrow. Til they came to the end of their laying life when they became broilers, no, boilers. A broiler is a hen that's probably been pushed on, killed early. A boiler is one that have been around for a long time. You needed to boil them to be able to eat 'em! Might've been a few capons about. We were pretty diversified. But about 1945, 46 the Duke of Somerset came down on a shooting party

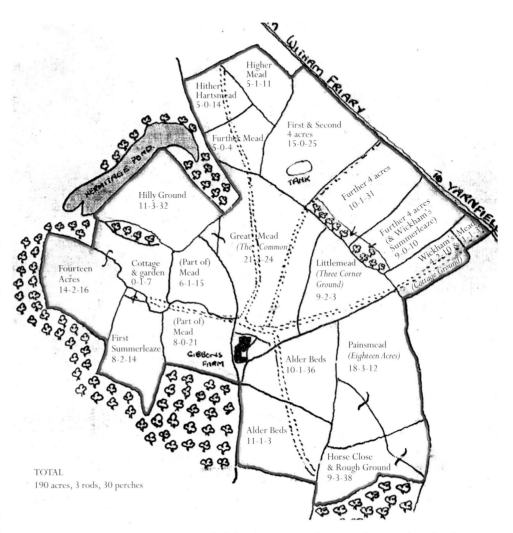

With field names added since, this map was included in the agreement for tenancy between the Duke of Somerset and Gordon's father, dated 28th July 1939. *"Father took over the tenancy at Gibbons in 1939, just over a month away from war. One hundred and ninety acres, £200 per annum."* Agricultural wages were £1/19/5 per week in October 1939

Gordon and his brother Brian fishing at the edge of the Common in the early fifties, with his sister Mary looking at the camera and Gill on the mat at her feet

and Father took the opportunity to point out the tiles on the roof of one of the cowstalls were slipping and needed some attention: "I'll get the agent to look into it." Well, the agent came back in due course and said if Father was willing to buy a milking parlour then the Duke would put up a set of buildings against the road at the top of the track to house the milking parlour. And they were going to build a new house there as well.

The new buildings went up, I think they became operational in about forty-seven or forty-eight, in that time period. And at that time, that was about the first purpose-built yard & parlour system in the country. You would still tie the cows up around the yard, bit of a halfway house but yes, you had a collecting yard, milking parlour, bedding yard – major step forward. Then in 1949 they decided that they didn't have enough money to build the farmhouse so they refurbished Gibbons. Put a Rayburn in

there and done the windows and generally made it habitable, because at one time mother had three children with bronchitis and pneumonia. Yeah, they shipped me off to Frome hospital, out the way! I wasn't that seriously ill but she'd too many to look after. The windows were six inch square panes, the wind and rain came in, not a great deal of heating – you had to be tough to survive!

The house at Upper Gibbons we built in due course but in the mean-time Father took the opportunity havin' two set-ups to become TT accredited. Before the cows moved up to the new premises we had a TT test – something like about thirty percent of them didn't pass and stayed down at Gibbons, until they were disposed of and the rest went up as a accredited herd to what became Upper Gibbons – well in due course, it didn't happen overnight – we had full accredited status and we thought TB was history. Having spent two months in hospital in fifty-four with what they thought were TB related problems it's a subject that's a little bit close to my heart. I came out of it with, well; I just can't straighten that arm but I met people in there that were far worse off than me because of TB.

On top of that we'd go round and double fence against all our neigh-bours so the cattle couldn't actually make physical contact [with other herds]. There was one instance where we shared a water trough with a neighbour, we had to fence that off and make other arrangements just to make sure.

I remember you telling me you had to sow Cottage Ground (*adjacent to Holt Cottages*) with brassica.

I sowed it with kale using a contraption called a pushbarrow which was basically a wheelbarrow with a twelve foot wide seed drill attached. I'd'a been about eighteen or twenty I suppose, summat like that. I done it in a day, five acres – going down was easy, but uphill – I can remember it now! There's history there in the field names: Dirtymead, across here you've got Little Thanks – Great Watermead, that speaks for itself – Oat Close, bit of good ground there, you need good ground to grow oats on. Greatmead, we always called that the Common. Littlemead – that's Three Corner Ground, there were two Painsmead, one belonged to Sweetnap, ours we called Eighteen Acres. This one, Alder Beds, which is split actually, two fields that is garden and eleven acres but we've got the old field [names] listed on Father's tenancy when he took over the farm in 1939.

Mother told me they were asked to grow oats in the war – but she said it wasn't really the ground for it.

The War Ag. came along and they would allocate so much land that you would have to grow corn. And sometimes you didn't harvest as much as you'd put in the ground.

So you were out there sowing kale. Was that a large proportion of your fodder crops?

No. Your main fodder supply then would've been hay from the farm. You didn't buy hay unless you were desperate. Father would never sell hay, either; wouldn't sell it, wouldn't buy it. Well, if he had to, he'd buy it but when he bought it it hurt so much, he didn't want to have to risk sellin' it and buyin' it again! But you were buyin' in cotton seed cake, various things like that for the cattle. There were two mills in the area then, there were Jones's at Bruton and Sheldons at Wells. Then they become Sheldon Jones and took over Bruton mill: and now they're all history anyway.

Kale was a good supplementary feed – the easiest way to feed it was to strip graze it. But Witham ground gets a little bit bottomless in the winter and you'd get chapped teats and lame cows, and whatever, so by and large we cut and hauled it to the cows, cut it in the field and fed it to the cattle in the yard – which had its own problems. We got five tractors stuck in one field one after the other. You'd keep trying to fish one out

then you'd get another stuck! That was down what we d'call Three Corner ground – we hauled jacks out there and sleepers and tractors there with spade lug wheels, steel wheels and you'd tie lengths, baulks of timber onto the wheels – all good fun! Of course, when I started farming, when I first remember the farm we still had a horse as well, just one Shire.

Silage wasn't in common use then?

No. Making silage in them days, wartime instruction booklets showing farmers how to make silage – one way was to get a tractor and plough (Standard Fordson tractor and a two or three furrow plough) and you ploughed a section of land where you were gonna make your pit and you worked the plough down through it and you got in there with your spades

Gill Read, Gordon's sister at Gibbons Farm with Smart, circa 1957. Gordon: *"That's Smart. That were the days when haymaking was very much a communial effort. All hands to the pump, and yeah. Good fun could be had..."*

119

and you shovelled it out the way then you ploughed more until you'd dug down and got a pit. The other way was the Nissen hut; well if you'd got the materials for the Nissen hut you could make a ring on the ground then you'd pile the grass and whatever you wanted inside the ring – trampled it down – after a lot of hard work. I mean, green grass is heavy!

Farmers knew about silage, they knew how to do it but the tackle to do it, the equipment just wasn't there; it was the muscle Mk 1 and it wasn't really adequate. If you lived next door to a vegetable processing plant then you might make efforts to ensile the greenery that came from there and then use it but hydraulic loaders and … but the invention of the buckrake revolutionised silage making – you went out with a mower and cut the grass, as you always had and you came along with a buckrake, picked it up! They had – even when there were horses about – green crop loaders that you hitched this gadget on behind a wagon and as you pulled it along it picked up the grass, shovelled it up and put it in the wagon and then you got it back to your hard dug pit, you shovelled it in. The end product, once you'd made your silage – then handling [it] after that was – you'd cut it out with a hay knife and you pitched it up with a pitchfork and it was about twice as heavy as if it was hay.

If you look at some of the old paintings of the harvest field, one thing you will see, something in there usually is somebody tippin' up a jar of cider – believe you me, you need the cider to be able to put up with the conditions under which you were working. So you always went to work for a farm that had good cider! Most farms would've had their own orchards and cider press, they had one down Moorpark – the orchard was already there, but having come up from Wedmore then cidermaking would have been [in the blood]. It's still in the family now. Roger [Wilkins at Land's End Farm, Mudgley] is a second cousin and he's about the biggest farmhouse cidermaker in the country now. Cousin Roger – used to go down there regular – since we've been down Wincanton I went down there, one Sunday I think, pulled in there and said

"Hello, cousin" – [he replied] "Must be Cliff's boy." He had me sussed in next to no time! Used to go down there [a lot]. First thing you had to do was to sample it: you'd sample the top house and then a sample from the bottom one, there you were gonna decide what you were gonna have; then, go in and see father and have a drop of whisky! An' when you come away, the rhynes seemed liked that (*gestures very wide*) and the road seemed like (*gestures very narrow*). Yeah, the good old days!

You were still making ricks post-war?

Oh yeah, we were making ricks up to 'round about fifty-eight, something like that and that's when Father bought the first baler. Aubrey Watts had the first baler that I can remember, that was a stationary baler, tied with wire. And you didn't have knotters, you had a bloke one side of the chamber and then you had the needles and you pushed them through and the bloke the other side pushed them back and wound the wire up and the bales, you needed a fork lift to pick them up – and there weren't no fork lifts! Aubrey was at Moorleaze farm – his son's still alive, saw him earlier today, Arthur.

The first tractor was in the fifties?

Before that. We had a Standard Fordson on rubber certainly by the end of the war. Gran'father had one then, that had high speed, a road gear on it and it were quite fast, but he would'a had that 1940, 41, early, and he had a combine ordered but it never came – everything was on licence, you just couldn't go and buy one, you had to make a case for it. And then the War Ag, they had a David Brown bulldozer on tracks and they used to go around ploughing. If you didn't plough it yourself – they'd come along and plough it for you, and then you'd get a bill! You didn' have a choice whether you were going to grow corn or not, if they decided you were going to grow corn and you were gonna do it it that field, then you either got on and did it, best you could, and if you didn't then the War Ag gang would come along and plough it and sow it and you'd get a bill.

An' when you come to sell what you'd produced you could only sell that through set channels. You couldn't just go and sell it on the open market, well, there wasn't no open market, it was all controlled. But sending cattle to market, they had to go to a designated market, all licences and whatever. There were a lot of ill feeling about being had over by the dealers – I can remember a lot of unhappiness about the system. I mean, I was only a kid looking on, mere whippersnapper!

Why did the Duke of Somerset leave Gibbons & Sweetnap [Farms] out of the main sale in 1954?

Partly because Charlie Hallett and his family had been tenants [at Sweetnap] since time immemorial and there was a reluctance to sell his farm from under him, so to speak. That was part of it, but there was also a piecemeal approach to the whole question of raising the funds for the death duties. Well, it were done in three stages. They sold off the village, part of the village in 1951.

After the estate incurred death duties (*Evelyn Seymour, the 17th Duke of Somerset died in April 1954*) they had to raise money. They decided to sell all the farms to the east of Holt Road, between Holt Road and Gare Hill as one lot. So that portion of the estate was offered as a single unit. It wasn't offered to the individual farmers. My grandfather, Charlie Stevens and a few other farmers (got a list of names somewhere) Sheppard brothers were involved, Miles, Jakins, they got together and formed a syndicate to put in an offer to buy the whole shebang. Not in the auction.

They wanted to pre-empt the situation by buying before the auction?

It wouldn't have gone to auction [anyway] because Cadbury's were in the market. Percy Quick, Cooper & Tanner's was acting on behalf of the syndicate. He was going round at ten o'clock at night, gone, gettin' signatures on the document from all the members of the syndicate, which he had to present in Rawlence & Squarey's office in Salisbury the following mornin' before ten o'clock because at ten o'clock Cadbury's were going to sign. And if they hadn't formed a syndicate, and if Percy Quick hadn't'a got the signatures in time, then the history of Witham would've been completely different. The syndicate bought it as a private deal; if they hadn't'a bought it, Cadbury's would have.

Before the day of the auction?

Yes, oh yes. If Percy Quick hadn't closed the deal that morning by ten, Cadbury's were gonna sign. It was as close as that. There was never a chance that it was going to public auction. There were some farmers that weren't involved in the syndicate that were a little bit miffed; but on the other hand (Percy Quick said to father years later) there were too many in it as it was because the more people you have in something like that, the more difficulty it is to act as a single unit. Prob'ly why Percy was having to go around late at night having to get those signatures. Anyway, the deal was done, the syndicate took their own farms and bits and pieces they wanted – Granfather, he took two woods, John's Planting and Chestnuts and a field that's opposite Nichollses [Holt farm], he took that. Walk Farm – Brian's father-in-law was tenant there – he couldn't or wouldn't buy. Sheppards the timber people bought that they stripped the best timber off of it and then sold it again, and it's been through various hands since then.

Perhaps it was a better offer than Cadbury's?

It may have been. I don't know if there was any preference given to the syndicate. If the Duke of Somerset had'n'a died then the Estate would've been kept together and it would've been different history again. If the farms had exchanged one landlord for another, Duke of Somerset for Cadbury's, then when the Duke's estate decided they needed to sell the other farms they wouldn't've been offered to the individual tenants, they would've been offered to Cadbury's. Cadbury's would've finished up with the whole Witham estate. You can't say with certainty but it would've been very likely.

So that left Charlie Hallett at Sweetnap, your father at Gibbons...

Nicholls at Holt, Aubrey Watts at Moorleaze, that's probably it. Because where Ron Ham is now [Lower West Barn Farm], that was Jackson's, that was already been sold off and when it was sold it was sold with a free water supply, which Ron Ham still exploits to this day – or his tenant does. Father was offered the opportunity to buy Gibbons round about 1955. I got a feeling the deal were done in July. They needed to raise extra funds, and they were left with the tag end of the estate. They kept Hicks Park Wood – they kept ownership of that, which they still have.

They were selling some cottages at Bradley in the 1955 auction.

Yep. About this time, Father could've bought Witham water supply for about a thousand pounds.

He didn't fancy the water business?

No, he didn't. Actually that was one of his major mistakes! *(much laughter)* If we'd had the idea of puttin' it into bottles then it'd've made more money than milking cows! Wouldn't've been very popular with the rest of the village, but yeah.

The single biggest failing with the Witham water supply was that there was not enough storage. That was down to the Duke of Somerset. Although a connection was made after the drought in 1976 to a spring at Trout Pond and then another in 2005 to the spring at Gare Hill, the storage was never increased. In my opinion, that pipe should never have come across from Gare Hill to the reservoir. It should've gone [direct] to Witham…and you would've had two independent supplies…it would've given a little flexibility to the system. if I'd still been associated with Witham I would've argued against it; as it is at the moment you've got one main, so if you've got a problem on that everybody goes.

The reservoir doesn't look much larger than a swimming pool.

It's not as big as a swimming pool – certainly not Olympic size, but it was built by GWR to service their railway engines – nothin' to do with supplying people with water. You look at the reservoir, look at the architecture. The whole thing was built for the railway cos it was a soft water supply. Witham village supply up until then came from Vicarage Hill, or as it was called prior to the vicarage being built, Panwell's Hill, the springs there – that was the water supply for the village and it was so hard you can nearly strike sparks off it.

The reservoir building in West End Wood was built by the Great Western Railway for locomotive water. Gordon: *"…nothin' to do with supplying people with water. You look at the reservoir, look at the architecture."* The classic GWR use of engineer's blue brick around the louvre opening shown here confirms his assertion

I don't know what the actual system of supply [then] was – the village as I first remember it had three stand pipes, and that was the water supply, connected to the reservoir, the present system. The pub would've had water laid on, both in the pub and in the cowstalls, the Clubroom, but most of the cottages you'd gone out with your bucket or pail and collected your water. You wouldn't've turned on a tap over your sink. No chance! There was one standpipe by the [former] Red Lion, one just above the pub outside Railway Cottages, one in the wall there and there was one round the other end of the village…tryin' to remember where it was, spect if you walk round there you'll find it there in the wall, an arch. There was also a standpipe outside Holt Cottages. Until we refurbished the cottages, round about 1960, 1961, when I got married, that was the only water supply – the standpipe outside. There were no supply into the cottages. I suppose that supply was put in around 1860, when the line was extended from Westbury to Weymouth.

As early as that you reckon?

I heard stories but it's way before my time and Father, family wan't even in the village at the time, but I heard stories that all the abled bodied men in the village volunteered their labour to dig the main in – it's not very deep in places! Some places it goes down as far as this room is high but other places he in't very far down at all. There would've been a deal done between the Duke of Somerset whose water it was, well the reservoir was built on his property, well it was all his property so there would've been cooperation.

Not all evidence is gone, but as you go down to Gibbons from Upper Gibbons, you cross over the stream that runs down the and walk down two or three hundred yards there used to be a concrete dam c'ross upstream which bayed the water back, fed it to a ram – two developments there, there's tanks back in the field, they're still there, brick built tanks that you can if you're brave and you've got a ladder you can go down and

have a look and then there were a later one I think, with filters and that for the ram, and then there was a glazed tile pipe ran from there across to supply Moorpark wi' water. That pipe can still be traced now if you know where to dig. Runs down by Holt and across past the bungalow. As you run up Moorpark track, the field there that's what they call Tank Ground and as you go to Moorpark and as you look it goes up to a bit of a hump, there's a tank there, and that water used to be pumped across from Gibbons to that tank and then fed on from there to Moorpark.

It isn't much more than a stream coming down from Trout Pond.

There's not that much water in it now; but when you consider the amount of water that's being taken out by the Witham water supply, you put that water back in the stream and (expresses quantity with his hands)…at one period in history I think, between Holt Cottages and Witham there were seven mills were on that stretch of water. Yes! They wouldn't've been very big, but I've seen a mill in Morocco – basically a wheel about four feet diameter, well actually barley they were grinding, a little family halfway up a mountain, and then they had a series of fields, not as big as this room but dug into the valley walls, they could grow three crops a year on that little patch. Lot warmer there, and they had a ready supply of water coming down from the Atlas Mountains. That was an eye-opener. And it would've been similar here, they wouldn't have been major mills but they would've been…get power where you can, when you can!

The electricity supply?

That came through in 1962. There had been various schemes put forward whereby everybody along the line would agree to pay so much and it would be based on your usage but nothing came of it because somebody would complain that they were paying too much and somebody else wasn't paying enough and there were a lot of talk: we all had generators of one sort or another but the year I got married they needed to reinforce the grid – partly because the quarries were growing and they put a link in from Bruton to Truddoxhill sub-stations. That's when we got electric!

We had a Startomatic [generator] down at Gibbons, at Upper Gibbons we had a diesel engine driving the vacuum pump and also driving a generator. I had a twenty-four volt system, lighting, nearly blew meself up on that! The engine was running twice a day for milking and then if you had a flat battery you would connect it up to the system, you'd be finishing it off in the morning, washing the plant through and you had nothin' to do for five minutes, "Oh yeah, there's that battery have been on charge, I'll take that off" – well, if you were overcharging a bit and you took one off and there was a bit of a spark, blew up – it happened!

Were there farm workers living in Holt Cottages?

There was a family, White, lived at no. 3: in fact they moved out when I got married in sixty-one. I went in there: Reg James and his wife – he worked for Colemans Quarry [at Holwell] – he lived in no. 4 and that's where Des was born. They were there until my brother got married, he's just coming up fifty years and Reg moved down to a council house down in the village and when Mrs James died Reg went into Frome. I can remember Reg; he couldn't get over the day they took [it] over. We refurbished both cottages and put a Rayburn in each one. Reg couldn't sorta get over the fact that turn on the tap and hot water keep coming out and he didn't need to put any in!

We take these things for granted now.

When I got married and moved in the garden had been neglected – Reg's half was tended to a (*gestures*) degree, but the other half was grass, like. Anyway, I went in with the weedkiller, sprayed it off, an' I went in with a garden rotavator and chewed it up; I put a bouter on the rotavator, bouted up the rows, got this sack of seed spuds, Reg comes and has a look "What ye reckon ye gonna get there, me boy?" So I said, "Hopefully

At Witham gymkhana in the field opposite the Seymour Arms, circa 1964. From the bottom right, Gordon pictured here with his sister Mary above and Ray Cary behind her. To Ray's right is Gordon's brother Brian and in front of him, Pete Cary

nothin' worse." I had a smashing crop of spuds! It were virtually virgin ground, hadn't grown anything for years, but Reg, he couldn't get over that for a time – that didn't seem fair!

That coincided with having a young family?

We got married in sixty-one. I bought a washing machine, oh crikey, the name of it, can't remember – it were the one that sorta revolutionised washing machines, the price was less than half of that of a Hoover twin tub. Anyway, I bought that, and I think we were actually switched on sometime in August 1962 and Bob [Gordon's son] arrived on the twentieth of September. 61/62 winter was average, 62/63 was the serious one. Des was still living next door and working at Frome police station, and he'd walk in on the railway to get to work and back. And Robert had a bit of problem, well he had to have special milk powder, Truelife or something like that. Des would pick it up in Frome and bring it back for Bess. Bob's six foot odd tall now – he survived.

Brian and Margaret [Gordon's brother and sister-in-law] moved into no. 4 Holt Cottages. We were in partnership until 'bout seventy-nine, I pulled out and ploughed my own furrow, so to speak. Went calf rearing initially and then we went on to finishing cattle, beef cattle. We left Holt Cottages round about when Gill got married, her fortieth anniversary was end of last December [2012], we swapped over with Mother and Father, they went up the cottages and Bess & I went down the farmhouse. 'Bout the same time we were building the house next door to the parlour [at Upper Gibbons] where Ian is now. Father gave me the choice of th'old farmhouse or the new one, and I opted for the traditional one. And y'know I still think I made the right choice as things panned out, yeap.

So your Father retired then?

No. Father stayed on. He was in partnership with brother and he was involved up until the time he had the first stroke and then he died in '86.

When we sorted out father's affairs and had deed of partition, he [brother Brian] had what he had and I had what I had, mother had what she had, that's when we put the [new] track [to Gibbons] in. The other one – the kids, when they were going to school, they used to ride their bikes and catch the bus up at the top of the track [at Upper Gibbons] and sometimes was a job to get the wheels to go around (mouths: 'cos of the shit').

So they'd drew up a new agreement – the old right of way (to Hicks Park Wood) was still there but in return the Duke of Somerset undertook to maintain the track. Well, I didn't know anything about it until after Father died – it all got resolved in the end but the Duke never did put his hand in his pocket for tarmac. No. They wanted to extract a lot of timber out of Hicks Park and they brought a chap down there who was going to haul it out and he took one look at the bridges and said "I'm not driving over that." So they had to put in new bridges. The arrangement with the new track made life a lot easier.

"Mother decided she didn't want another tenant and that's when she had the two cottages turned into one house." With the kettle on the hot plate of the Rayburn ready for the next pot of tea; here is Gordon's mother Mary Stevens at Holt Cottage in May 1999 - pictured shortly before moving to Frome, sixty-one years after her wedding (see photograph on page 62)

Here's a photograph your sister gave me – *'Home inventions to make haymaking easier 1960s/70?s'* Is that your Nuffield?

No. That started out life as a van labelled 'Dog's Delight' – it delivered dog food, well, pet food. And Bill Marsh [the garage at Kilmington] had it up there. We bought it and we stripped it down, you can't actually see from there but it had two gearboxes, one behind the other to get the speed

Gordon on the van converted in their own workshop with brother Brian looking on, 1973

so then I done that job cos there was a firm up Keynsham that dealt in fork lifts, hired them out and one thing and another and I could get the masts off of scrap fork lifts – I mean, that was the secret. Once you had that bit, then makin' up the rest, convertin' the rest was quite simple. All made in our own workshop. I used to spend hours in there, fiddling.

The lorry in the picture, you were hauling then?

Initially we had a lorry to haul Father's point-to-pointer. But obviously it had to do a bit more than that! So we hauled our own feed and stuffs and we hauled hay and straw and all the rest of it an' then when lorry regulations were tightened up, plated and tested and whatever – Bill Powell was doing the coal round and there was no way his own wagon was going to pass th'MoT – Bill wanted to retire from farming anyway. We took over his farm and rented it, which continued up until quite recently, and we hauled his coal, delivered his coal for him until he sold it to Rose's of Gillingham.

Was the Nuffield was the first tractor you bought?

No – Father bought that December 1958; and that continued in the same ownership until I sold it and come down here [Wincanton]. It spent a lot of it's time with a rear loader on it – ah, there it is! Yep. There it is with a rear loader on, which was very useful for cleaning out sheds and what-ever; and then after we started using the bale packer an' that, decided to convert it into a fork lift. I turned everything around, turned the steering round, gearbox round, turned it into a rough terrain fork lift. So it went on… *(gestures at picture)* that's Ian [Stevens, Gordon's nephew] up there, Sandra [Gordon's daughter] there, Brian there, and Bess. I done some of my courting on that tractor. The Missis, I took her baling!

down, gear it down so's it was useable – going that way you could get it down so it would creep along, going that way *(gestures away from bales)* it would do fifty, sixty miles an hour! I got my wife to drive it up the road once *(long pause)*. Only once! We bought a bale packer which would stack the bales in packs of twenty, automatically, and then we needed the 'quipment to be able to handle it. [The photo above] that's at Upper Gibbons, when we were all working together. The date there would be seventies. I think first year we had the bale packer was seventy-two or three, round that period – in the sixties we were still chucking 'um out by hand, bale by bale. After we had that one, then that was after Bill Powell's old coal lorry, a Bedford, I converted that to start with but that had a petrol engine in, used to run it on TVO an' that but he sorta died,

Gordon's Nuffield tractor: *"There it is with a rear loader on, which was very useful for cleaning out sheds… that's Ian [Stevens, Gordon's nephew] up there, Sandra [Gordon's daughter] there, Brian there, and Bess. I done some of my courting on that tractor. The Missis, I took her baling!"*

Would you have stayed on farming longer if Foot & Mouth [in 2002] hadn't occurred?

Foot and Mouth stopped me. Stopped me dead in the tracks. Cos we had for some years… round about ninety-four, I suppose; we'd basically switched from just calf rearing to finishing cattle right the way through, we were doing barley bulls, we were also buying cattle, store cattle, in Frome Market and finishing them out on a barley ration and yeah, we were doing very nicely, thank you! Initally, when we started we were returning summat like forty percent on the gross, on the money, over about a six week period; from the time I bought the cattle 'til we cashed them would'a been about six weeks. As time went on it got a little more difficult; price of corn went up, price of beef went down, and the price

of cattle went up a bit, but we were still making good money, and then, Foot & Mouth came along – closed the markets down. I couldn't buy in the cattle to replace what we were putting through. Eventually I could go out to the farms and buy direct from the farmer – that's not the same as standing in the market and bidding – that's different. I just wasn't cut out for it. Y'know. I'd go to market, look round at what cattle were there, I knew what I wanted; I knew what I was prepared to pay; and I bid accordingly and if my bid wadn't enough, tough! When you go onto somebody's farm, and start to buy something from them that they've nurtured from this [a young age] and you've been in the same game yourself: I couldn't, anyway; some people could – but I couldn't drive the bargain I needed to make the profit. And then…price of property went up; I said to Bess one day, "If we cashed this place in" – there was a place called Darkharbour at Templecombe that went on the market and made what everybody thought at the time was silly money. And I said, "If we could sell for something like that" – invest the money – I mean you could get five percent or something like that then without any trouble at all, "we'd be making more money than we are now." So she said, "What we doin' [here then]?" So Foot and Mouth was the major catalyst; if foot and mouth hadn't come along we'd'a continued buying the cattle, finishing them – and how much longer I'd'a done it, I don't know. But that was the key catalyst plus all the rules and regulations that came along in the wake of the outbreak, largely because even though we'd all been there before, we'd all been on the sharp end of Foot and Mouth, we all knew what needed to be done, but we had a government that didn't know its arse from its elbow. We knew we were in trouble after the first week. I was talking to somebody, he said "What d'ya think?" I said "It's just a question of sitting tight until it gets to you." And for a lot of people it was just that. We were lucky round here, very lucky. After that the fun had gone out of the job and as I said property prices went up – so we sold.

Tell me about the Friendly Society, Gordon.

Basically the rules that are still in place now (but not adhered to) are the rules amended round about 1918, thereabouts. The people that became members of the Friendly Society had to be under forty to join. If you were over forty you weren't a good enough risk – you could be a member above the age of forty but you had to start before. Worked out about a pound a year that you paid in; the Society would employ a doctor who would administer to anybody who was sick or injured; they would also pay out so much a week for a limited period to people that were sick; and they paid a death grant to widows of members that had died; and every fifth year they would have a break year. Have a dinner, a massive supper and all the accumulated funds would be distributed back out to the members. Then at every Whitsuntide they had the Whitsun feast and they would go to the vicarage, get the vicar out down to hold a service at the church then parade to the Clubroom, Seymour Arms and have their supper. Prior to that they went to the Red Lion. There are books that date back to 1760, lists there of menus of what food they provided, how much it cost, a bit of social history…these days it just carries on as a piece of living history.

A lot of Friendly Societies evolved into today's insurance companies. Witham and Priddy, they still operate one. And it's break year this year!

Did you ever get a payout?

When I was in hospital with the elbow (*points to scar*) when I was about fourteen.

So you were paying in even then, as a child?

[It's] family tradition that gran'fathers put their gran'sons in to the Friendly Society as soon as they were born. My gran'son, I pay his wack

every year, yeap. Years ago, there would've been a monthly meeting and people would've paid in monthly. There was a box with four locks on; all different; four keys, secretary had one, and there were three trustees, each had a key of their own. So they all had to be present to open the box. One break night p'raps twenty or thirty years ago, doesn't matter – but as an exercise, we projected up to today's values. The equivalent that they were handling on break night was in excess of thirty thousand pounds, if you brought up the average wage from the contributions from the 1918 rate to the present day. So no wonder there were four locks on there, yes! If they'd stopped having that break and returning the funds every five years they'd very soon accumulate big resources. They wouldn't pay out in the case of venereal disease, though – you had to be a good boy!

The circus vehicles – how did they come to be there?

Well, we'd converted the cowstalls – what is now (or was) Summerleaze, we converted it into a calf rearing unit for export calves. So we'd buy in second quality calves that weren't fit to travel, fit for export, and we would keep them about thirty days and advance them until they were ready to go, mostly to France, sometime to Italy, but France was the main market. It was twenty-four calves in a room, on slats, centrally heated, air-conditioned, quite a set-up. And it worked. Our mortality rate all the time we were runnin' it was about nought-point-six percent which… [is] not bad, believe you me for calf rearing. Then the job disappeared. The whole trade changed, and basically the French were coming over, buying the calves and taking them straight away without any advancing. Anyway, our business as far as that went finished, so we've got this shed, which is redundant, and we'd got heating in there and we ripped out all the crates. So we approached Mendip District Council, Malcolm Williams, Economic Development Officer. An' he come out and had a look and…well at one stage we were set to have a recording studio – an' that didn't happen, then we were set to have a paper making set-up, and that

Circus vehicle and digger awaiting removal after Gordon quit Gibbons, winter 2002

didn't quite happen, nearly did – next thing we know there's a circus looking for a summer workshop. Right? Send 'em along! We met some very interesting people, that were the next few years, it was several years they were operating. Initially they came there and they were using the sheds and making their props an' that; not quite sure if that were the first year but somewhere along the line they come down and put their big top up and rehearsed their show. That's when they were Captain Bob's Circus, with Maxwell painted as a caricature on their lorry. Anyway, they rehearsed their show, got it together an' then they invited all the kids and everybody from the village up to our preview, so we had a circus show on our hands, and then they took it on tour. Went up to Bristol, Bath and they finished up one year they went down to Spain, no, down to Italy, but that didn't work out very well cos the trailers they had, they actually had forklift truck tyres on these trailers to take, Ifor Williams trailers to take the weight, yeah, they'd take the weight. What they couldn't take was the temperature! It's a bit hot in Italy.

They come there, I mean that year and the next when we had the Mamas and Papas come after that, a different circus but with some of the ones from before – they stored their vans there but they wouldn't be living there other than when they were rehearsing their show. They'd be there and they'd come and go and it gave you an entirely different insight into human nature – there'd be a knock at the door and there would be this scruffy individual that probably hadn't bathed for a month;

Brian Stevens (left) and Gordon Stevens pose for the photographer having finished stacking bales using the van Gordon had converted. Upper Gibbons Farm, 1973

dressed in a collection of clothes; and he'd open his mouth and it'd be pure public school. We had quite a cosmopolitan band down there and we never had any trouble at all. They were a great help along the way as well. We had a bit o'clearing up to do afterwards… but when we found out that caravans burn quite well, that solved a lot of problems! But, I tell ya, if you're going to burn a caravan, first ascertain whether or not it's got a fridge in it. Fridges go bang, quite spectacularly! Then before the circus, we had the naturists. For three or four years – might've been longer. Cos at one time, they were all set to build a clubhouse down in Spencers…I don't know how they could stick the flies. Naturists, they would tell you that they're free and easy, free of life's cares, and woes and all the rest of it…you never met such a bunch of hung-up individuals in all your life. Talk about neuroses! But they were pleasant enough, in their own way.

The Mamas and Papas, they wanted a water supply and they were camping up the lane – turn in the yard and go up left. Go on up and out in the gate in the field. But anyway, I'd dug a trench up through, run the water pipe up from the barn, and ticked it all up to a water trough, left it on all night and left it filling. Well then, about six o'clock the next morning, I goes out an' and walks the line of the trench up, make sure there weren't any leaks. And there was this young lady from Columbia, she's quite generously endowed, and she's there doing her morning ablutions at the water trough…Ha! Took me a while to get over that one. There was another one, Tina I think, they had this knife thrower and they asked me if there was any timber there they could make up a backstop, where the knifes were thrown. I said, well there's some pallets there, help yourself. So anyway, bang bang bang, and they had a go. Bloody knives were about that long *(gestures 18 inches or so)*, coulda been a bit longer. This girl was standing there against the board like that and this guy would *(gestures knives thrown around outline of figure)* and there would be somebody there holding the board up! Pallet wood

130

i'n't that very good, bloody knives were coming through… they said "Do you think we could have some more timber?" I said "I think you better had"…we didn't actually kill anybody.

Funny how life twists and turns around. The naturists certainly opened your eyes to a different world; but the circus people, they were something else – you'd meet the family, you know, this one's by him, and this one's by him, and this one's by him, it was Willow, and Strange. Been meaning to go to Hay on Wye cos one of them sort of packed the job in and went to open a bookshop there some years ago, but how he got on [I don't know].

We had a full blown circus show! There were at least thirty or forty people came up from the village, free circus show! Yeah, they weren't bad, they were pretty good. One of them, Ben, as far as I know is still running the circus school up Bristol now. Happy days!

Gordon Stevens in retirement. Wincanton, April 17th, 2015

GLOSSARY OF LOCAL TERMS

Aisle up the stooks arrange the corn stooks in straight lines during harvest

Arrold up stuck on barbed wire/caught up

Bail (milking) wheeled trailer for milking cows in the field, e.g. during summertime

Barton cowyard

Bit of a strop on getting quite cross, e.g: *'he had a bit of a strop on'*

Boughten shop purchase, e.g: *'I boughten that today in Frome'*

Chamming chewing (e.g. a pie)

Clegfly horsefly

Cocked out living out in the sticks

Cocky gate makeshift gate made from wire and posts

Come a gutser fell off, e.g. motorbike

Creeping on, going on leaving

Cuss flashes to be very angry

Cussed I off he/she told me off

Daddiky feeling poorly

Dapping along getting a move on, e.g: *'I were dapping along'*

Diggered covered in something, e.g. chicken pox or mud. Messy

Dimpsy/dumpsy twilight, just getting dark

Dumbledore bumblebee

Dunch stupid person

Dung putt two-wheeled tipping dung cart

Dunnum? don't they?

Ensile process of making silage

Emmet (batch) ant(hill)

Evet newt

Fourgrain pick four tine dung fork

Frank heron

Gammy handed wifter left handed person

Gert big, great, very

Going on leaving

Gone back person or livestock looking more poorly than before

Goosegog gooseberry

Granfer gravy/Chuckypig/Granfycroocher/Granfergreg/Pill bug wood louse

Hangings, danglings sloping field

Hen fruit eggs

How be on, you? How are you?

I can mind a time I can remember when

Iss it's

Led in bed (I was) lying in bed

Mangelwurzels root vegetable for animal fodder, machine for preparing same

Marlpit quarry for marl stone used for building

Mommet scarecrow

Oh ah yes

Pitching snow settling

Polly dish wash pied wagtail

Poor man's velvet cider and port

Pretty chicken poacher's term for a pheasant

Puds hands, e.g: *'ee got gert puds on en'*

Quarr quarry

Rhynes drainage ditches on the Somerset levels

Skittered off left, leaving

Shard hole in the hedge big enough for livestock to escape

Shippon cowshed

Shrammed feeling cold

Smeech thick smoke e.g. bonfire

Stick kindling

Straps small strip of land, typically used for a cow & calf, or a sick cow.

Tallet loft

Thas that's

Thic this, that

Truck, Truddoxhill Trudoxhill (neighbouring village to Witham Friary)

Trugged it up lifted it up, made vertical, e.g. a post

Tunneger funnel

Work it into 'n swallow, put in, rub in

Work some off remove liquid from container

Woss what's

CONTRIBUTORS

Stella & John Hill interviewed on 22.11.11 at Yew Close, Witham Friary by Deborah Liggatt and Chris Featherstone. Transcription by Josh Teasdale, transcript edited by Chris Chapman.
Ron Harding interviewed by his daughter Julie at Castle Cary in 2009. Transcription by Julie Harding, transcript edited by Chris Chapman.
Roy Wheeler interviewed on 18/24.11.11 at home in Frome by Helen Nicholas & Gordon Teasdale/Mike Gorman. Transcription by Josh Teasdale, transcript edited by Chris Chapman. Further editing by Chris Chapman.
Mavis Walker interviewed on 23.08.13 at home in Witham Friary by Chris & Roy Featherstone.Transcription by Josh Teasdale, transcript edited by Chris Chapman.
Geoff & Ann Sheppard interviewed on 08.10.14 at Quarr Hill Farm, Witham Friary. Interview, transcription & transcript edit by Chris Chapman.
Don & Doris Stevens interviewed on 28.11.11 at Toll House Farm, Tytherington by Martin & Ann Howard. Transcription by Josh Teasdale, transcript edited by Chris Chapman. Additional interview on 10.10.14 by Chris Chapman at Toll House Farm, Tytherington. Interview, transcription & transcript edit by Chris Chapman.
Margaret Trussler interviewed on 01.03.13 in Witham Friary by Mike Gorman. Transcription by Josh Teasdale, transcript edited by Chris Chapman.
Norman Crouch interviewed on 19.09.13 at Grazemoor Farm, Witham Friary. Transcription & transcript edit by Chris Chapman.
Duncan Gale interviewed on 02.02.12 at Yew Close, Witham Friary by Mike Gorman. Transcription by Josh Teasdale, transcript edited by Chris Chapman.
Brian Bullock interviewed on 03.04.13 at home in Frome by Mike Gorman. Transcription by Josh Teasdale, transcript edited by Chris Chapman. Additional interview on 08.06.15 by Chris Chapman;transcription & transcript edit by Chris Chapman.
Melvyn Walton interviewed on 23.08.13 at home in Frome by Mike Gorman. Transcription by Josh Teasdale, transcript edited by Chris Chapman.
Robert Ludgate interviewed on 09.01.12 at Rough Stubbs, Witham Friary. Interview, transcription & transcript edit by Chris Chapman.
Gordon Stevens interviewed on 11.09.13 & 17.04.15 at home in Wincanton. Interviews, transcription & transcript edits by Chris Chapman.

Thanks are also due to John and Stella Hill for suggesting and starting a list of local terms; Keith Dicker, Geoff Sheppard, Gordon Stevens and others for further contributions to the list; Lorna at the Seymour Arms for helping with names of people and places; Adrian Vaughan; Amy Frost; Nancy Garnett-Thomas; Andrew Miller; Mary McQuillan; Michael McGarvie; Vi Norman; Martin & Ann Howard; Will Palmer; and all who have supported the Witham Friary History Project since its inception.

PHOTOGRAPHY CREDITS

Front cover: © Adrian Vaughan
Half title: courtesy of Seymour Arms
Opposite title page: Extract of Ordnance Survey 1:25,000 maps, 1957/8
Foreword: courtesy of Don & Doris Stevens
p10: © Scholastic Souvenir Company
p13, 14, 15,16, 19, 21: courtesy of Stella & John Hill
p18: courtesy of Seymour Arms
p20: Civil Defence Leaflet, 1963
p22: Seymour Arms yard, 1960s – courtesy of Seymour Arms
p23 & 25: © Chris Chapman
p27 & 33: courtesy of Julie Harding
p35 & 38: courtesy of Roy Wheeler
p39, 41, 55: © Chris Chapman
p45, 46, 48 & 51: courtesy of Geoff Sheppard
p47: courtesy of Linda Sheppard
p56, 60, 61, 63, 67 & 69: courtesy of Don & Doris Stevens
p62: courtesy of Gordon Stevens
p71 & 72: © Chris Chapman
p75: courtesy of Michael McGarvie
p77: courtesy of Chris Chapman
p79: courtesy of Liz Kefford
p81: courtesy of Chris Chapman
p82, 83 & 85: courtesy of Norman Crouch
p87, 88 & 93: © Chris Chapman
p90 & 92: courtesy of Duncan Gale
p96: courtesy of Stella & John Hill
p97: outline by Chris Chapman
p100: courtesy of Liz Kefford
p103: © Chris Chapman
p104, 105, 107, 108, 109, 111 & 122 courtesy of Robert Ludgate
p113 & 114: © Chris Chapman
p116, 117 & 118: courtesy of Gordon Stevens
p119, 126: courtesy of Gill Read
p122: © Chris Chapman
p124, 127 & 130: courtesy of Gordon Stevens
p125, 129 & 131: © Chris Chapman
Rear cover: courtesy of Liz Kefford & Gordon Stevens

INDEX

(numbers in bold indicate photographs)

air raids: Filton, 31; Bristol, 32
Alfred's Tower, 74
Allen, Horace, newspaper delivery, 24
Austin, Mrs, shopkeeper, Upton Noble, 29

Baker, Alf, **107;** Barry, 102
Batcombe, 78
Beeching's axe, 14
Bullock, Beryl, 52, **96,** 97, 102
Bullock, Brian, **93,** 93-99, **96;**
    father averts disaster for the
    Cornish Riviera express train, 98
Bullock, Maggie, 102
bus service, 14, 24, 44, 52

Cannon, Meryl, **85**
cars: Citroen, Hillman, 30
Cary, Peter **96, 124;** Ray, **124**
catching the train: to Shepton 35;
    to Weymouth 37;
cattle, breeds of: Ayrshire, 67, 97;
    Friesian, shorthorns 16; milking,
    16, 23, 30, 39, 46, 49, 54, 58, 64,
    67, 83, 86, 95; dairy herd at Quarr
    Hill, 48; moving from Cheddar to
    Witham on the train, 57; picking
    up calfs from the Eavises, 58;
    icicles forming on coats in the
    1947 winter, 39, 64
Cheddar Valley line, 98

cheese making at Tynemead, 52, 97;
    delivery to Crump & Way, 97;
    Barber's of Ditcheat, 97
Chilcompton, 45, 47
church choir, BBC live broadcast of, 95
cider, 37, 51; making of 58;
    drinking at Moorpark, 90
Compton, 'Gramp', **100,** 101
Coombes, Peter, 43
Cox, Arthur, **16,** 21, 96; Catherine
    (Kitty), **19, 96;** Dave, 110, **111;**
    Maurice, on motorbike, **15;** Vi, **15**
Crees, Timmer, 51
Crickham, 58
Crouch, Mrs, 79
Crouch, Norman, 79, 81-86, **87;**
    moving away from Hinckley Point 82;
    horse breeding, 84
Cruse, Bob, signalman, 103
Cunard Line, 99
Cunnington, Mr, **96**
Cunnington, Mrs, teacher, 13, 14,
    64, 91, 94

Deacon, Fred & Ron, 59
Dibben, Alan, 52
Diener, Otto, 33, **33**
Douel, Pete, **1,** 113; Jean, 19, 43, 113
Dovecot: history of, 8; as a youth
    club 17; photograph of 1927-28
        football team outside, **18;** listing, 44

evacuees, 43, 59, 90, 94

farmers: Cary, 15; Gartell, 52, 66;
    Harding, 27, 31; Hoddinott, 68;
    Jackson, 35, 36; Jakins, 52, 99,
    98, 102, 121; Jowett, 14, 19, 21,
    43, 52, 95, 99; Nicholls 106-108;
    Sheppard, 45-55, 78, 121; Stevens,
    35, 46, 57-71, 84, 115-131;
    Watts, 118, 122; Yeoman, 19, 43, 52
farms: Barrow Hill, 50; Baycliffe,
    Maiden Bradley, 116; Bellerica,
    purchase of, 28; Gibbons, 115-118,
    circus vehicles at, 129; Grazemoor,
    30, **82;** Higher West Barn, 19, 95;
    Home Farm, Stourton, 73-76;
    Homemead, 66, demolition of, 70;
    Horsehill, Evercreech, 31;
    Land's End, Mudgley, 120;
    Laurel Farm, Maiden Bradley, 65;
    Lower West Barn, 19, 95, 122;
    Little West Barn, 35, 84, 116;
    Manor, 19, 52, 66, 94, 99, 116;
    Millers, 14; Moorleaze, 19, 98,
    110, 120, 122; Moorpark, 57-68,
    90, 102, 116, 120, 123;
    New House, 48, 52, 94; Quarr
    Hill, 45, Seymour, 23; Sweetnap,
    46, 119, 121, 122; Tynemead, 19,
    45, 52, 95, 98, 102; Upper Gib-
    bons, 118, 123-126; Upper Holt,

7, 46, 110; Walk, 19, 98, 121;
    Witham Hall, 68, 106, 109;
    Witham Park, 15, 57
feed mills: Jones at Bruton and
    Sheldons at Wells, 119
field names: Plough Field,
    Marlpit, 32; Dirtymead, 118;
    Oat Close, Greatmead (the Common)
    Littlemead (Three Corner Ground),
    Painsmead, Alder Beds, 119
football teams; Witham, 47, 92, 110;
    Maiden Bradley, 92;
    Butler & Tanner's, 92;
    Wallington Westons, 92
Friendly Society, 23, 128

Gale, Fred, **18;** Duncan, 18, **88,** 89-92;
    motorbikes, 92; Karen, **85,** 89;
    Kevin, **88,** 89; Roger, 106; Val, **92**
Gare Hill, 16, 24, 43, 90;
    water supply from, 121, 122
Gingell, Gladys, **62, 116**
Glastonbury festival, 58
Gould, Jeremy, **111,** 112;
    John, **111,** 112; Richard, 112
Green, William, 116

Hallett, Charlie, 121, 122
Harding, Ron, 27 -33; with sister
    Madge, 28; future wife Mary, 32;
    father Graham, **33;**

marriage, sale of livestock, 33
Harrison Cripps, 98
Hermitage Lodge, 109
Hill, John, 13-25; on motorbike, **15**;
  early working life, 15; under-age
  drinking, 17; in pub garden, **25**
Hill, Stella, 13-25, outside school,
  13; at Littlewoods, **14**;
  express train stops for her whilst
  heavily pregnant, 15;
  in pub garden, **25**
Hoare, Sir Henry, 73
Holt Cottages, 91, 115, 123-125;
  electricity arriving at, 124
Home Guard: 7, **21**, 31, 37, 50, 90;
  fire watch at Cranmore Tower 51;
  horses, working: Flower, Janet, 16;
  Smart, 16, **119**; Shire, 35;
  at Moorpark farm, 61, **63**;
  ploughing and carting, 76;
  at Holt Farm, 106; at Gibbons, **119**
Hunt, Miss, teacher, 13, 59, 64, 101
hunting 78, 84, 108;
  killing badgers, 108;
  digging a fox out of a rick, 109

Jackson, Anthony, **96**
Jagger, Chris, 58
James, Des, 124
James, Reg, **18**, 124

Keeper Day, 108
Kerry Croft, 21, 68, 110
Kerslake, Dick & Betty, 110; Michael, **96**
Kilmington, 78, 108, 125
Klaxon, Cold War, 20

Land Girls, 37, **107**
Longbridge Deverill, 27, 28, 116
Longman, Billy, 99
Ludgate, Robert, **105**, 105-110,
  107, **111**; in Madagascar, **112**; **113**;
  mother Christina, **104**

Maiden Bradley, milk round, 65
Mann, Captain, 84
Marsh, Bill, 124
May, Jimmy, **96**; Sue, **96**
Miles, Cynthia, 106

National Service, 38
National Trust, 75
Naylor, Linda, **96**; Patsy, **96**; Val, **96**
New Friary Cottages, 43
Nicholls, Alice, 106, **109**; Bernard,
  106; Bert, **107**; Edna, 106; Fred, 106,
  107, **109**; Fred (grandson), 109;
  Jess, 109; John, 50; Len, 106;
  Mary, 106; Philip, 106
North, Bert, 94
Nunney, 13, 14, 17, 22, 31, 89

Panwell Hill, 122
Phelps, Mrs, calling the doctor, 14;
  needlecraft, 17
Phelps, Paul, 68
Phillips, Kath, 64
Pill, 105
Powell, Bill, 46, 68, 126; Marcus 109, **111**
prisoners of war, draughts board
  made by, 36; working on farm, 36
Private Drive, 66, 74
Proctor, Harry, **107**, 109; Ron 43

Read, Gill (née Stevens), **118**, **119**

Quick, Percy, Cooper & Tanner
  auctioneer, 33; organising farmer's
  syndicate, 121

Salvidge, Herb, **18**, 19; cows of, **22**
Savin, Mr, blacksmith, 97
schools: corporal punishment in, 64;
  Frome Grammar, 14; Keyford
  College, 29; Kilmington, 74,
  Oakfield, 106, Sexey's, 91, 101, 106;
  Shepton, 35, 94;
  Sunny Hill, 14, 101; Upton Noble,
  28; Wanstrow, 106; Warminster,
  46; Witham, 8, 13, 35, 42, 52, 64,
  94, 101, 116
Severn Tunnel, 98

Seymour Arms, 8, 17, 23, 25, 31,
  37, 43, 62, 88, 113; lunches at, 44;
  Friendly Society meeting
  in Clubroom, 128
Sheppard, Ann, **51**; Danny, **111**, 112;
  Geoff: 45-55; grandfather, **45**; father
  with brothers, **46**; Geoff at school,
  47; father in yard, **48**, with son Will,
  55, in football team, **111**; Len, 45,
  46, 47, 50; Reg, death of, 49; Tom,
  52; Will, 53, **55**
signal box: Blatchbridge, 40;
  Brewham, 36, 81; Cranmore, 103;
  Witham, 103
Singer, John, 33, **33**
Smallpeice, Sir Basil, 99
Snook, Elsie, 73
Somerset, Duke of: auction, 7, 121;
  water supply, 22, 120; opening
  fete, 43; letting Gibbons Farm, 115;
  letting Holt farm, 106; letting
  Laurel Farm, Maiden Bradley, 65;
  letting Tynemead Farm, 45;
  shooting party in 1945, 117;
  reservoir built on his property, 122;
  dispute about track maintenance, 125
Stevens, Bess, 125, **127**; Brian, 68,
  110, **118**, **124**, 125, **126**, **127**, **130**;
  Charles, **62**, **67**, 116; Cliff, **56**,
  wedding of **62**, 67, 100, 120;

Don, 6, 56, 57-71, in the harvest field 61; pageboy at brother's wedding 62; on cart horse 63; wedding 67; 71, 116; Doris, catching moles, 65, 67, 71; Gordon 68, 106, 114, 115-131; sowing Cottage Ground with kale, 118; silage making, 119-120; foot & mouth, 127; Ian, 127; Joan, 62; Les, 62, 67; Mary, 124; Mary (née Gingell), 62, 125; Phil, 70, 111, 112; Ren, 64, 68, 102; Sandra, 127; Vi, 62

Stourhead House, 65, 76, 77
Stourton, 73-78
Strap Lane, 81, 84

Taylor, Mr, village shop, 14
Thane, Anna, 96;
Thane, Gill, 96;
Thane, Mr, 96;
Thane, Mrs, 86, 96;
Toton, Rich, 111, 112;
tractors: International, 16, 49;
   Ferguson, 52; Allis B, 56, 60;
   Standard Fordson, 119; David
   Brown, 120; Nuffield, 126, 127
Trollope, Herbie 46
Trout Pond, 122
Trussler, Margaret, 72, 73-79;
   21st birthday party with RAF
   officers from Zeals aerodrome, 76
Truddoxhill, 14, 124

Upton Noble, 14, 28-30, 32, 35-37, 110

Vicarage Hill, 102, 122

Vicars: Reverend Prince, 9;
   Pescod, 42; Hodder, 42; Dunn, 94;
   Bawtree-Williams 94, 96

wages: Arthur Cox, 16;
   Brian Bullock, 95, agricultural, 117
Walker, Mavis, 41-44;
   retired from Kenya 41
Walton, Melvyn, 101-103, 103
Wanstrow, 22, 31, 32, 49, 89, 106, 108, 112, 117
Warren, Annie, 68, 110
Warren, Flo, 59, 68, 93, 110
Warren, Fred, 103
wartime: bomb dropping on
   Hermitage lake; 94; D-Day, 37, 94;
   Green Howards fight with GIs
   outside pub, 7, 37;
   planes: Spitfire, 32;
   Flying Fortress, 32; Dornier, 32;
   Anson crash landing at Marlpit, 32;
   seen whilst at school, 36;
   Hurricane crash landing in
   Postlebury, 50; rationing, 36
Wase, Dennis, 68
water supply: GWR reservoir, 122;
   between Gibbons and Moorpark, 123
Wedmore, 58, 116, 120
Wheeler, Harry, 96; Hubert,
   entering Belsen, 38;
   Roy, 35-40; in his pedal car, 35;
   in Benghazi during National Service, 38;
   in Witham village hall, 39;
   Sandra, 96; Wilf, 107
White, Arthur, 35; Derek, 35, 106;
   Jackie, 96;

Wilkins, Roger, cidermaker: 58, 120
winter of 1947: 39; 64; train getting
   stuck in snow at Doulting, 94;
winter of 1963: 15, 40, 52, 68, 124
Witham Friary:
   auction by Estate, 7, 57, 99, 121-122;
   church choir, BBC live broadcast
   of harvest festival, 95,
   Christmas service, 96, 102;
   cottages, No. 42: 13, 20;
   No.44: 14, 19; No 49: 101;
   No. 51: 93; Binden, 35;
   Rough Stubbs, 59, 89, 90, 93,
   110; Kerry Croft, 110;

council houses, Littlewoods, 13, 102;
football team: 1927-28, 18;
   1979-80, 111;
   pitch at Moorleaze, 110;
   Friendly Society, 128;
gymkhana, 78, 79, 124;
railway station, 7, 9, 14, 15, 29, 37, 40, 50, 52, 77, 90, 94, 95, 98, 106, 109; loading milk 69, 76;
   obliteration of, 109;
   railway workers, 98, 103;
   train to Weymouth, 29, 37, 106;
   unloading cattle 57;
school life, 64, 91, 94, 101;
youth club, 17

Lemon Beer - A refreshing drink for workers in the hay field.
A recipe from a book started by Gordon Stevens' grandmother